GACE

Business Education

SECRETS

Study Guide
Your Key to Exam Success

GACE Test Review for the
Georgia Assessments for the
Certification of Educators

Dear Future Exam Success Story:

Congratulations on your purchase of our study guide. Our goal in writing our study guide was to cover the content on the test, as well as provide insight into typical test taking mistakes and how to overcome them.

Standardized tests are a key component of being successful, which only increases the importance of doing well in the high-pressure high-stakes environment of test day. How well you do on this test will have a significant impact on your future, and we have the research and practical advice to help you execute on test day.

The product you're reading now is designed to exploit weaknesses in the test itself, and help you avoid the most common errors test takers frequently make.

How to use this study guide

We don't want to waste your time. Our study guide is fast-paced and fluff-free. We suggest going through it a number of times, as repetition is an important part of learning new information and concepts.

First, read through the study guide completely to get a feel for the content and organization. Read the general success strategies first, and then proceed to the content sections. Each tip has been carefully selected for its effectiveness.

Second, read through the study guide again, and take notes in the margins and highlight those sections where you may have a particular weakness.

Finally, bring the manual with you on test day and study it before the exam begins.

Your success is our success

We would be delighted to hear about your success. Send us an email and tell us your story. Thanks for your business and we wish you continued success.

Sincerely,

Mometrix Test Preparation Team

Need more help? Check out our flashcards at: http://MometrixFlashcards.com/GACE

TABLE OF CONTENTS

Top 20 Test Taking Tips

1. Carefully follow all the test registration procedures
2. Know the test directions, duration, topics, question types, how many questions
3. Setup a flexible study schedule at least 3-4 weeks before test day
4. Study during the time of day you are most alert, relaxed, and stress free
5. Maximize your learning style; visual learner use visual study aids, auditory learner use auditory study aids
6. Focus on your weakest knowledge base
7. Find a study partner to review with and help clarify questions
8. Practice, practice, practice
9. Get a good night's sleep; don't try to cram the night before the test
10. Eat a well balanced meal
11. Know the exact physical location of the testing site; drive the route to the site prior to test day
12. Bring a set of ear plugs; the testing center could be noisy
13. Wear comfortable, loose fitting, layered clothing to the testing center; prepare for it to be either cold or hot during the test
14. Bring at least 2 current forms of ID to the testing center
15. Arrive to the test early; be prepared to wait and be patient
16. Eliminate the obviously wrong answer choices, then guess the first remaining choice
17. Pace yourself; don't rush, but keep working and move on if you get stuck
18. Maintain a positive attitude even if the test is going poorly
19. Keep your first answer unless you are positive it is wrong
20. Check your work, don't make a careless mistake

Business Law

FMLA, Drug Free Workplace Act, OSHA

The Family and Medical Leave Act was passed in 1993. It enables employees to take up to twelve weeks of unpaid leave for certain family or medical emergencies without risking the loss of their job. This law was created because of the tendency of employers to be rather callous in dealing with employees who have legitimate personal crises. The Drug Free Workplace Act allows employers to discipline or terminate employees who are using or distributing controlled substances in the workplace. The Occupational Safety and Health Act requires employers to meet certain standards regarding safety in the workplace. OSHA also created an agency to survey businesses and ensure that these standards are being maintained.

Sexual Harassment

Sexual harassment is any inappropriate verbal or physical conduct of a sexual nature, specifically when it is directed at an individual because of his or her gender. The Supreme Court has determined that sexual harassment violates the protections for employees that were set forth in the Civil Rights Act of 1964. There are also state laws against sexual harassment. In order to prove that sexual harassment has occurred, a plaintiff must be able to demonstrate that the alleged harassment was either severe or consistent enough to affect their work, and that the employer is liable because of their knowledge of the harassment. In many cases, the courts have leveled extremely harsh punishments against businesses that neglected to stop or punish sexual harassment.

Quid Pro Quo and Hostile Work Environment

Most sexual harassment cases are either built on the idea of *quid pro quo* (literally, "this for that") harassment or the existence of a hostile work environment. In order for a plaintiff to prove that *quid pro quo* harassment has occurred, he or she must be able to demonstrate that harassment was considered a necessary part of keeping the job, that tolerating harassment affected his or her progress in the company, or that the harassment clearly affected his or her ability to work. In order to make the case that harassment created a hostile work environment, the plaintiff must prove that he or she was discriminated against on the basis of gender, that this discrimination was pervasive and regular, that he or she was negatively affected by this discrimination, that any reasonable person would have been similarly affected, and that management either knew or should have known about the harassment and did nothing to stop it.

American Tort Law

The American legal system divides actionable torts into three categories: intentional torts, torts of negligence, and strict liability torts. Intentional torts are those made on purpose by the tortfeasor (the person who committed the tort), and include battery, assault, false imprisonment, fraud, defamation of character, and malicious prosecution. Torts of negligence are the most common form of tort in the American legal system. Common examples are malpractice, emotional distress due to negligence, and product liability. Strict liability torts are brought after injuries resulting from ultrahazardous activities, for which the tortfeasor can be charged even without having been negligent. Most tort claims are heard in state courts.

Teaching Ethical Decision-Making

Unfortunately, making ethical decisions in the business world is often quite difficult. Business teachers should recognize this fact, and equip their students with a good decision-making process. The first step in the process should be defining the problem; students may often jump to conclusions about a problem without ever really articulating it. Next, students should be trained to consider the various alternative solutions to the problem. Making a list on paper is a good way to externalize choices. After this, students should get in the habit of identifying the consequences of the various proposed solutions. Consequences may be both short-term and long-term; as every businessperson knows, losing a customer in the name of short-term profit is always a bad decision. Finally, students should determine whether they have enough information to make a decision, and if not, they should have the discipline to acquire the information they need.

Labor Unions

A *labor union* is a group of laborers organized to promote their common interests. Unions are found in most industrialized countries. Their primary goals are to improve compensation and working conditions. Union membership has declined considerably in the United States over the past fifty years; today, only about 16 percent of the labor force belongs to a union. The actions taken by unions often set industry standards that affect even nonunion laborers. Unions pursue their goals by recruiting new members, negotiating with management, working to promote legislation favorable to their cause, and even organizing strikes and work stoppages if necessary. Unions often have remarkable political strength, which has occasionally been exploited by their leaders.

Communication

Basic Rules of Business Meetings

Business meetings are essential for maintaining the flow of information through the company, and for making sure that lines of communication are open between the various members of the team. Face-to-face meetings are better than emails or phone calls at defusing potential conflicts. In order for a meeting to be effective, however, there must be an acknowledged agenda. There must also be one person who is charged with administrating the meeting: that is, keeping control, steering conversation, making sure accurate notes are taken, and following up on the decisions that are made. Meetings may be called for any purpose in business: motivating, team building, setting goals, making decisions, clarifying policy, or just checking in with one another's work.

Priorities and Desired Outcomes of Business Meetings

When a business meeting is being planned, the priorities and desired outcomes of the meeting must be taken into consideration. Establishing the priorities of a meeting simply means establishing why the meeting is being called in the first place. A list should be made and ordered by importance; if resolving the prioritized issues is not worth the time spent in the meeting, perhaps it is best to wait. After determining why a meeting is to be held, the desired outcomes of the meeting should be enumerated. Some meetings will aim at making a decision, while others may be held just for the purpose of continuing a discussion. Meetings may be held to describe a new point of company policy, or to listen to a guest speaker.

Sequence and Timing of Business Meetings

When the agenda for a business meeting is being planned, the most important items should always be placed first. Anything that absolutely must be covered in the meeting should be among the first things discussed. Many business managers try to avoid putting several controversial items in row when planning a business meeting; they seek to defuse conflicts between attendees. In a similar fashion, the meeting planner should determine how long the meeting will need to be, and about how much time should be devoted to each particular item. Long meetings need to be furnished with a break so that participants can maintain their attention. Many business managers have discovered that "working lunches" tend to add too much time to meetings and make it hard for participants to stay focused.

Date, Time, and Venue for Business Meetings

When planning a business meeting, one should try to select the date, time, and venue that are most congenial to the participants and appropriate to the task of the meeting. A meeting's date should cause as little disruption for the participants as possible. This is especially important to consider when calling people from different departments of a business, because these people may be operating on different schedules. Many meeting planners have decided that long meetings should be held either at the beginning or the end of the work day, so that travel time can be minimized. Finally, it is essential that the venue for a meeting have ample seating, whatever technological aids will be required, and access to refreshments, and that it be a reasonable distance from the workspace of all required participants.

Basic Strategies for Public Speaking

There are a few basic public speaking strategies that can allow even the shyest individual to present him or herself well in front of a crowd. First, it is essential to know both the room and the audience. This makes it possible to tailor one's speech and manner appropriately. Next, a speaker should know his or her material well. It is always a good idea to try and relax before speaking. Many speakers find that it helps them if they visualize their speech beforehand. During a speech, one should never apologize for being nervous or for any other problems; simply try to remedy these problems as quickly as possible. Finally, a good public speaker concentrates on his or her message rather than on him or herself.

Speaking Aids

There are a number of technological aids for public speaking currently available. Probably the most popular of these is the PowerPoint computer software, which allows the user to create elaborate slide systems that can be projected onto a large screen to accompany a speech. The same equipment used to project PowerPoint presentations can be used to project web page or word processing documents. Many speakers enhance their speeches with audio or video footage, which can be manipulated and presented using basic computer software. Besides these more advanced forms of equipment, many speakers still use such old-fashioned props as overhead and slide projectors.

Economics and Finance

Inflation and Deflation

Inflation is the rate of change in the price level. Although most economies exhibit rising price rates every year, there is occasionally a reduction in price level, known as deflation. Inflation does not necessarily mean that every price increases, only that the average price has increased. Demand-pull inflation is when greater demand results in inadequate supply and raised prices. Cost-push inflation results when increases in the cost of production lead to supply shortages across the economy, again leading to a raise in price. The two major problems associated with inflation are economic uncertainty (people are unwilling to make long-term investments because of the perceived instability of the market) and the random distribution of wealth that results when price becomes so variable. Such a distribution of wealth may not be in the best interest of society.

Recession

A recession is typically defined as the economic situation in which a nation's gross domestic product has diminished in each of the last three quarters. A recession often leads to falling prices, which can lead to a depression (an extended recession, basically). On the other hand, a recession may lead to a sharp rise in prices, creating a condition known as stagflation. In most developed economies, recessions occur every five or ten years, although many economists suggest ways that governments can smooth the cycle. Recessions are typically caused either by shocks to the economy or by a downturn in investment because of a lack of consumer confidence. Often, a series of negative events send a national economy into a downward trend that eventually becomes a recession.

Monopolistic Competition

In a market displaying monopolistic competition, there are a number of firms (fifty or more) selling slightly different products. The difference between products may be more perceived than actual in this model. Product differentiation is often just a matter of special packaging or advertising. Because there are so many sellers, entry into the market is relatively easy for new firms, and there is very little direct competition between firms. Since there is a degree of difference between products, firms have a little bit of control over price, and will typically produce the quantity of product that maximizes profit at the price they set (known as equilibrium output). This sort of competition is probably the closest any real market will come to perfect competition.

Oligopoly

In the market structure known as oligopoly, a small number of interdependent firms compete for market shares. Since there are only a few firms in the market, any change in price or output by one of the firms affects all the other firms. It can be very difficult for new firms to enter an oligopolistic market, because they usually depend on ownership of large amounts of raw materials, or access to specialized technology. Examples of oligopolistic market include the auto and steel industries in the United States. Most of the time, the firms in an oligopoly operate on what is known as an economy of scale: that is, the more units they produce, the more the cost per unit goes down. There is always the danger of collusion (when competing firms agree on prices and output to maximize profit) in an oligopoly.

Monopoly

In a monopoly, there is only one firm. Obviously, a firm holding a monopoly has a great deal of control over price; they may charge whatever price maximizes their profit. It is impossible, usually for legal reasons, for another company to enter the market. There are a number of ways in which monopolies arise. One way is through the patenting of a new product to which the inventor has exclusive rights (in the United States, these rights last for seventeen years). Sometimes the government creates monopolies by giving a certain firm exclusive rights to a product. Other times, the market for a product is only sufficient to successfully sustain one firm. This is called a natural monopoly, and is regulated by the government. Monopoly is the exact opposite of perfect competition.

Supply and Demand

Supply and demand are the two factors that determine price. Supply is the desire and ability to sell a certain amount of goods at a certain price, within a given time period. Supply may fluctuate depending on price and the quantity of goods being sold; that is to say, supply is a measure of the goods available at a certain price, not just the quantity of goods in existence. Demand is the willingness to buy a certain quantity of goods at a certain price, in a given time period. A simple economic graph is often drawn to illustrate the relation between supply and demand. In it, the demand curve slopes such that a greater quantity is being demanded when the price is lower, and the supply curve shows that producers will make more goods as the price for those goods rises; the equilibrium point, where these two lines intersect, is the level at which producers will be content to produce a certain amount for a certain price, which consumers will also be willing to pay.

Balance of Trade and Balance of Payments

No country wants to be dependent on foreign imports, and so governments impose tariffs, quotas, and other trade barriers in an attempt to aid domestic production. In doing so they are always mindful of the balance of trade: the difference between the value of the nation's exports and its imports. Every country aspires to export more than it imports. For the most part, the United States has had a favorable balance of trade over the past century; however, at some points an increase in military spending, foreign travel, and foreign aid have resulted in an unfavorable balance of payments: the difference between a country's total payments to other countries and the payments that country receives from abroad. Economists are split as to whether this balance of payments needs to be closely minded, or whether the United States would do well to help other, smaller economies.

Comparative Advantage

The economic principle of comparative advantage suggests that every country should produce whatever it can produce most profitably, without trying to emphasize total national self-sufficiency. According to this idea, the nations that operate according to their comparative advantage will get the most out of their people and natural resources. This includes scenarios in which a focus on one profitable good means the country must import goods which it could also make more economically at home. For instance, advocates of this theory argue, doe sit make sense to add a 50% duty to products that Japanese manufacturers can produce for half the cost? Wouldn't it make more sense, they argue, to find those products that American firms can produce more economically and export them?

Calculation of Unit Cost

Businesses calculate average unit cost in order to determine just how much it costs them to produce a single unit for sale. This number is essentially an average, and is found by adding together all of the manufacturing costs incurred during a particular period, and then dividing this total by the number of units that were produced during that same period. It should be noted that manufacturing costs include the costs of materials and labor, but not other business expenses, like employee insurance or executive salaries. Some businesses that have a long-term production process may have to add up a number of partially-competed products as fractions of whole units.

Price Increases and Decreases, Price Elasticity of Demand

A change in price is usually calculated as a percent, meaning that the difference in price is divided by the original price and multiplied by a hundred. For instance, if a candy bar cost $0.75, and then the price increased to $0.85, the price increase would be calculated 0.1/0.85 x 100, which equals a price decrease of about 12%. Change in price is often used to determine price elasticity of demand, the change in demand for a particular product based on changes in its price. Price elasticity of demand is calculated by dividing the percent change in the quantity demanded by the percent change in price. The price elasticity of demand of a certain item depends on how many competing goods exist, the level of consumer income, and whether the good is considered to be a luxury or a necessity.

Simple Interest

It should be very easy to calculate simple interest, which may apply to money deposited in a bank or money borrowed from a bank or another lender. Only three factors are needed: principal, rate, and time. The principal is the amount originally deposited or borrowed; the rate is the percent of the principal that is added as interest; and the time is simply the number of years (since the interest rate is usually expressed as an annual rate) the money has been deposited, or the time over which the loan will be repaid. Simple interest, then, is calculated by multiplying these three factors. For example, if $100 dollars has been in the bank for 2 years with a 3% rate of interest, it has now become $106.

History and Purpose of Deposit Insurance

Because banks cannot both lend money and keep on hand the amount equal to all deposits, there is always the danger that if all the depositors asked for their money back at once, the bank would not have enough to comply. This scenario actually happened in the United States during the Great Depression. To prevent it from happening again, the United States government created what is known as the Federal Deposit Insurance Corporation, to provide insurance to banks on their deposits. Every national bank is required to carry deposit insurance, and most state banks do, as well. Deposit insurance has virtually eliminated any massive runs on a bank's funds; often, though, FDIC policy is to have a healthy bank take over the operations of one that has been hit hard by withdrawals, rather than to issue money directly to the struggling bank.

Public Market

The public market is the collection of thousands of individuals and groups of investors who buy and sell corporation stocks and bonds. Groups of investors may include pension funds, insurance companies, investment trusts, mutual funds, commercial banks, savings banks, loan companies, businesses that invest in other businesses, government agencies, and investment banks. Indeed, many people who have life insurance policies or pensions do not even realize that they have funds invested in American business. Universities, hospitals, churches, and other charitable organizations also frequently invest in business. Most American corporations get their money from the public market, and prefer to do so.

Value of the Public Market

Obviously, the public market aids business by providing funds for financing operations and growth. The public market provides a number of other services, as well. For one, the ease with which securities can be bought and sold encourages a level of investment that otherwise would be difficult to imagine. Moreover, the constant sale of securities means that investors will always have a good idea of what their securities are worth. Smaller businesses that do not sell stock may have more difficulty assessing their own value. Even better, the public market gives business an immediate appraisal of their recent actions; if the public has confidence in the direction the business is moving, the stock's price will rise. In this way, the pubic market acts as a metric for corporate decisions.

Common Stock and Par Value

Corporations may sell either common or preferred stock as shares in ownership. Typically, common stock entails the right to vote on the members of the board of directors, as well as the right to a share in the corporation's profits when dividends are divided, and a share of the corporation's assets should they be liquidated. The share of liquidated assets is divided from the total remaining after creditors and preferred stockholders are paid. Each share of stock has a par value: a dollar amount that is supposed to have been given to the original purchasers of the stock. Of course, stock with a par value of $100 may have an actual value much lower, depending on the success of the corporation. Indeed, many stocks no longer carry a par value, as it is almost impossible to sell common stock for less than the stated par value.

Corporate Bonds

Corporations often raise funds by borrowing money and giving corporate bonds or notes in exchange. Bonds are evidence of debt that a corporation agrees to pay to a particular group of creditors. When issuing bonds, corporations agree with a representative of the lender, called a trustee, as to what the terms of the bond will be. Corporations may promise not to pay dividends should earning dip below a certain level, or they may agree not to borrow any more money without the consent of that lender. Bonds may be held for any length of time, although there is usually an established time by which they must be repaid. Until a bond is repaid, the lender receives interest, a small percentage of the total amount the corporation has borrowed.

Different Types of Bonds

There are a number of different types of bonds. Many lenders desire some guarantee of repayment, and so bonds are often secured by some piece of valuable property. If this property has a mortgage placed on it, the bond is called a mortgage bond. If stocks and bonds from other companies are held as security of repayment, the bond is called a collateral trust bond. Most bonds are simple debenture bonds, in which the only security offered is the general assets and earnings of the corporation. These bonds are called sinking-fund bonds when the borrowing corporation promises to pay back the bonds slowly. Occasionally, corporations will issue bonds that are eligible to be traded in for common stock at any time: these are called convertible bonds.

Investment Banks

Investment banks do not do any of the things that commercial banks do. Rather, they make money by marketing new issues of stocks and bonds to the general public, pension funds, insurance companies, or other large investing institutions. Investment banks may facilitate the entry of new securities into the market by underwriting them: that is, buying them all and agreeing to sell them to the public, thus guaranteeing their legitimacy to any prospective buyers. Most of the time, underwritten securities are sold almost immediately after they become available. Occasionally, an investment bank will agree to sell securities on a best-efforts basis, meaning that they will try their best to sell but are making no guarantees. Of course, this is not the preferred position for corporations.

How Investment Banks Help Business

Investment banks provide a great service to businesses by making their stock known and available to a broad selection of potential investors. Without investment banks, businesses would be left to sell stock to the people they are in close contact with, or to unknown buyers with uncertain financial histories. Investment banks act almost like department stores, buying inventory from manufacturers and then employing specialized workers to sell it again. For the most part, however, investment banks are too expensive for small companies, who will find it difficult to have much success with a small batch of stock on the public market, anyway. The services of underwriting may be as much for a small issue as for a large one. Furthermore, investment banks prefer to make large issues, so that they can quickly determine the appropriate price.

Brokerage Houses

Brokerage houses are organizations that buy and sell securities on behalf of investors. Brokerage houses are essential to the market because they specialize in knowing who owns what stock at what time; if a single investor, for instance, wanted to buy one hundred shares of a certain stock, it could take that investor an extremely long time to find someone who owns that stock and would like to sell. Almost all investment banks also operate as brokers, and most investment banks have divisions handling transactions of already-issued securities. Brokerage houses make their money by charging a commission on purchases and sales. This commission is usually modest for a single share of stock, but it quickly expands with the thousands of transaction made by brokerage houses every day.

Security Exchanges

Security exchanges are locations where members of the exchange come together to buy and sell securities among themselves. To be a member of the exchange is known as "owning a seat" on it. Typically, brokerage houses will own multiple seats on an exchange. The best-known security exchange in the United States is the New York Stock Exchange (NYSE). The general public is forbidden from making transactions on the floor of this and other exchanges in the United States and worldwide. Security exchanges make their money from the charge for membership; they do not themselves engage in the buying and selling of securities. Members are allowed to sell their seats if they choose to do so, as long as the buyer is approved by the security exchange.

Listed and Unlisted Stocks

A listed stock is any stock that a stock exchange has authorized to be bought and sold. There are certain requirements that most exchanges have for listed stocks. If a stock is only bought and sold by brokers and small retailers, and not through the facilities of any security exchange, it is considered unlisted stock. It used to be that listed stocks were strongly preferred by investors, because of their supposed stability and because it was easy to find out their selling price. However, it has become increasingly easy to discover the value of unlisted stocks, and so the only real advantage now offered by organized exchanges is some prestige and a minimum listing standard. There is some speculation that the growing efficiency of the over-the-counter market may someday render the exchanges obsolete.

Security Exchange Members

The members of security exchanges typically fall into one of four categories. Commission brokers are the largest group of exchange members. They maintain offices near the exchange and handle transactions both for non-members and for other exchange members, receiving a commission on the transactions they aid. Registered traders buy and sell securities on their own behalf, hoping to make a profit out of avoiding commissions and receiving first-hand information from the exchange floor. Some traders focus on one specific area of security exchange; these traders may work for others or on their own behalf. Odd-lot dealers are those who specialize in making transactions in units of less than a hundred shares. They receive a commission for buying and sharing these smaller lots for other members and non-members.

Securities Investors

Anyone entering the stock market will function either as a speculator or as an investor. An investor is one who buys stocks for long-term use, rather than in the hopes of taking advantage of temporary price changes. Investors are usually trying either to ensure the safety of the money they invest (known as the principal), to earn money from the investment by means of dividends or interest, or to see the investment increase its value. It is rare that the same investment can satisfy all of these conditions at once; that is, the stocks and bonds that have the best chance to increase dramatically in value usually carry a greater degree of risk, and the safer stocks and bonds are unlikely to accrue much value in a short time.

Safe Investments

For investors looking to ensure the safety of their principal, the best investment is a deposit in a savings bank or the purchase of bank certificates of deposit. There is also a great deal of security in government bonds, though these cannot always be drawn out when an investor would like. The market value of a bond is determined by its interest rate, the current market rate of interest, and the date on which the bond can be redeemed. Investors buy bonds with an eye towards their yield, the amount of interest plus the payment they can expect when the bond is redeemed; if this amount is less than investors can get for other government bonds, it will be difficult for the investor holding the bond to get rid of it.

Annual Return

It is quite common for investors to select stocks and bonds in the hopes of getting the highest possible annual return without sacrificing safety. If interest rates are very high in a given year, there will be plenty of stocks and bonds that offer excellent returns without putting the principal in jeopardy. Even when interest rates are lower, good public utility stocks often increase steadily throughout the year. For the most part, bond yields will be higher than dividend yields for good stocks. This is because stock investors usually anticipate that the stock will increase in value as the market improves or as the profits of the company increase. For this reason, they are willing to accept a lower dividend yield.

Potential Increase in Investments

Many investors are less concerned with the dividends they will receive than with the potential increase in the value of the company. These investors look for a growth stock or for a bond that can be converted at their discretion into common stock. Oftentimes, stock can be sold for a high price even when it has not paid out any dividends at all. Stable, fast-growing stocks will have a high price/earnings (P/E) ratio, the market price per share divided by the annual earnings per share. If this ratio is high, it reflects the market's confidence in that company. Price/earnings ratio tends to be self-fulfilling; that is, companies with high ratios tend to continue their success, while those companies with a low P/E ratio may have a difficult time reversing a negative trend.

Company Performance

Obviously, investors are taking a risk when they put money into a company. There is always the chance that the company could go bankrupt, and that investors could thereby lose their entire stake. Stockholders therefore feel justified in expecting payment for the risk they take, as well as for the use of their money. Company managers have a similar interest in getting the highest possible return for their investors; the rate of return on equity (that is, the percentage of earnings after taxes to stockholder's equity) is the way that they determine the success of their company. Indeed, the price/earnings ratio and the rate of return on equity are essentially measuring the same thing, because high profits and continued investment are dependent on one another.

Speculation, Bear Markets, and Bull Markets

Securities speculation is the attempt to make money from very short-term and temporary fluctuations in the price of stocks and bonds. Depending on supply and demand, security prices are constantly moving up and down; successful speculators are those who can correctly anticipate changes in the attitudes of investors and therefore predict price movements. They must continually find stock that is either overvalued or undervalued. Of course, it is difficult to make a very large profit on speculation in any one transaction. Instead, speculators hope to accrue their earnings from a long series of mostly correct decisions. Some speculators are able to make money in a bear market (when most stock prices drop), though most find more success in a bull market (when most stock prices go up).

Option Trading

Option trading is a type of security transaction in which options (contracts that give the holder a right to buy or sell certain shares of stock at a certain price over a certain period) to buy or sell stock in a company are exchanged. An option to buy shares of stock is known as a call option. An option that requires another buyer to purchase one's stock at a specified price is known as a put option. Option trading allows speculators to gain the rights to much larger pools of stock than they would be able to if they had to buy each share outright. This means that they have the chance to increase their earnings when they correctly guess changes in the market. Those who sell options to speculators benefit, too, in that they receive the price of the options.

Securities and Exchange Commission

The Securities and Exchange Commission is an American federal government agency that protects the interests of the public and investors during the issuing and sale of corporate securities. The SEC is led by five people appointed by the president. These individuals serve for five years at a time. Over the years, the SEC has influenced the government to pass laws transferring the burden of quality from the buyer to the seller of securities. The SEC closely supervises stock exchanges and brokers to prevent them from taking advantage of unwitting investors. Of course, the work of the SEC does not prevent investors from losing their money; it only seeks to ensure that when they lose money, they do so fairly.

Borrowing on Credit

Credit, from the Latin word meaning "to trust," is the willingness of the seller or lender to allow someone else, be it an individual or a business, to have something now and pay for it later. Unless the borrower has a sterling credit record, the lender will usually require that something else be offered as security, to be given to the lender if the borrower cannot make payments. Companies may use a variety of assets as security when they borrow money on credit. The business may offer securities or accounts receivable, or they may give the lender assurances of assets they hold in warehouses (shown by warehouse receipts), or assets currently in transit (shown by bills of lading). Indeed, anything that could ever be resold is eligible to serve as security.

Promissory Notes

A promissory note, sometimes simply called a note, is a promise made by the borrower to repay the lender the sum of money that has been borrowed, along with a specified amount of interest, after a certain amount of time (or on a certain date). Promissory notes are common instruments of credit for businesses borrowing money from banks. Dealers of goods or services may also accept notes instead of money. Promissory notes are often negotiable, meaning that the lender can sell them to someone else, who then has the responsibility for collecting the loan. Some notes are sold with recourse, meaning that the buyer can demand payment from the original lender if the borrower fails to repay the money.

Drafts

One of the more common instruments of credit is the draft, an order made by one party (the drawer) to another party (the drawee), telling it to pay a certain amount to a third party (the payee). Drafts are different from promissory notes, in that they are an order, rather than a promise, to pay. Regular checks are considered a form of draft: when an individual consumer writes a check to the supermarket, for instance, he or she is essentially telling his or her bank to pay the supermarket a certain sum. In business, drafts are typically used when the seller doesn't want to give credit to the buyer, and demands payment before the buyer takes possession. This is often the case when the buyer is from a different country, or has an uncertain credit record.

Demand Drafts and Time Drafts

There are a couple of different drafts that are used as credit instruments. A demand (or sight) draft is one that is payable as soon as the seller (the payee) presents it to the bank (the drawee). Regular bank checks that bear the current date are demand drafts; once an individual has written a check to a retail store, for instance, that check may be immediately deposited. A time draft, on the other hand, is payable at some predetermined future date. Drafts do not even need to be made out to a specific payee; if it is just made out to the bearer, then it can be deposited by anyone that has it. This is done just as an individual might make a check payable to cash. This is often the case when the draft is written by one member of a business and given to another to give to the appropriate, as yet undetermined seller.

Acceptances

Trade (or bank) acceptances are a special form of time draft. They are written up by the seller and sent to the drawee, who then accepts them as binding by signing his or her name. At this point, the acceptance becomes a negotiable document; that is, it can be bought and sold. If the acceptance is taken by a business firm, it is called a trade acceptance. If the bank takes the acceptance, it is called a bank acceptance. For the most part, the use of acceptances is restricted to the sale of goods. Acceptances are easily negotiable when they are accepted by individuals or businesses with excellent credit ratings. In these cases, even the Federal Reserve Banks will buy acceptances on a discount basis.

Certified Checks and Cashier's Checks

Most of the time, businesses will accept a check from an individual or company without any guarantee of its validity, as long as it is for a relatively low amount and is from a reputable bank. However, in some cases the payee needs more reassurance. In these cases, businesses or individuals may acquire certified checks or cashier's checks. To create a certified check, the bank simply stamps the word "certified" on a regular check and immediately deducts the amount from the individual or business' account. It is then apparent to the payee that there are sufficient funds to cover the transaction. Cashier's checks are written to the payee by the bank itself, and charged to the individual or business' account. Assuming the bank is reputable, the payee will accept the check.

Line of Credit

Generally, businesses borrow cash for a short period in order to finance accounts receivable, inventories, and other short-term operating costs. If a company needs to borrow funds for a short time, it will go to its bank and ask for a line of credit, the right to borrow up to a certain amount of money over a period of time. Assuming that the business is in good standing, the bank will consider it a good credit risk and will grant the credit. Most of the time, no security is involved in this kind of arrangement. Of course, the bank will request some kind of summary of the business' accounts, so that it can make an accurate assessment of how much cash the business is likely to need and how much it will likely have available in the future to repay the loan.

Revolving Credit and Compensating Balances

Sometimes banks will guarantee a line of credit to a business for a long time, a service known as revolving credit. The bank will charge a slightly higher interest fee for revolving credit. The higher interest rate compensates the bank for the inconvenience of keeping a large amount of money ready should the business need it. Banks may also require that a borrowing business keep some minimum amount of money in a deposit account. According to banks, this compensating balance is required because it makes sense for borrowers to be depositors as well. It seems more likely, though, that compensating balances are required because they allow banks to charge deceptively high interest: if a business borrows and pays interest on $1000, for instance, and has to deposit $150, it is as if they had only borrowed $850.

Present Value Theory

Investment analysts use present value theory to account for changes in the value of a sum of money over time. The present value is simply the amount of money one has today that will be worth a given amount at some future date given a certain rate of return. If, for instance, one has $620, and one is guaranteed a 10% rate of return every year, then in five years that $620 will be $1000. The present value is $620 and the future value is $1000; investors use this calculation to show how much a given investment is likely to accrue over time, and to illustrate the gains that can be made through sound investment and patience. Even more astounding is the difference between present and future value when compound interest (interest that accrues both on the principal and on the interest already earned) is accrued.

Risk Management

Risk management, for businesses and individuals, is the effort to identify, consider, and make the most efficient defense against various types of risk. In investing, risk management specifically is the practice of assessing the likelihood of loss and making adjustments to ensure that the potential for loss is tolerable to the investor. Some investors are uncomfortable with great risk, and are willing to sacrifice the chance for great gain to avoid danger. Investors who seek to avoid risk often purchase government bonds, which tend to be relatively stable, rather than corporate securities. If an investor can stand to lose his or her investment, however, he or she might gamble on some potentially lucrative stocks.

Factoring Companies and Commercial Finance Companies

Factoring companies act much like commercial finance companies, with one important distinction. Factoring companies purchase accounts receivable from businesses at a discount because, unlike commercial finance companies, they take the loss if the account remains unpaid. Since they are taking a higher risk, they receive a greater discount. Of course, factoring companies are very selective in the accounts that they will purchase. Factoring companies also occasionally lend money to businesses, with the business' inventory as security. Factoring companies are usually only used by small companies; larger firms tend to finance their credit through commercial banks. Financing through factors may give a business the reputation of not being solid enough to borrow from commercial banks.

Fiscal Policy

Fiscal policy is created and implemented by the federal government in the hopes of increasing the gross national product, raising employment, and stabilizing prices and money. Fiscal policy may be either expansionary or contractionary. *Expansionary policy* is designed to combat a recession and consists of either lowering taxes or increasing government spending, whereas *contractionary policy* aims to fight inflation and involves raising taxes and decreasing spending. It should be noted that such actions are an example of discretionary fiscal policy, which is an explicit and purposeful adjustment of the economy rather than reliance on the "invisible hand" of market correction. Any results of fiscal policy are usually reflected in the national debt.

Monetary Policy

Monetary policy comprises the actions of a central bank or currency regulation organization that affect the size of the money supply and, thereby, affect interest rates. Monetary policy is designed to restrain inflation, improve the employment rate, and generally stabilize the economy. Monetary policy is either expansionary or contractionary, depending on whether it seeks to enlarge or diminish the money supply. In the United States, monetary policy is carried out by the Federal Reserve in three ways: through open market operations, through the discount rate, and through reserve requirements. To halt a recession, the Federal Reserve typically tries to expand the money supply. Conversely, when inflation is too great, it attempts to limit spending by contracting the money supply.

Monetary Policy of the Federal Reserve

The monetary policy of the Federal Reserve System may be promoted in three ways: through open market operations, through the discount rate, and through the reserve requirements. Open market operations are the most common means of adjusting the money supply and consist of the government's purchasing and selling of government securities to affect the size of bank reserves. If the Federal Reserve wants to increase the money supply, it will buy securities, thus putting money into the economy. The discount rate is the rate of interest the Federal Reserve charges for loans to banks. Adjustment of this rate will either encourage or discourage bank borrowing. Reserve requirements are the levels of reserve funds that the Federal Reserve requires of banks. Adjusting this amount may affect the money supply, although this method is used much less frequently than open market operations or the discount rate.

First and Second National Banks of the United States

The First and Second National Banks of the United States are the historical antecedents of the current Federal Reserve System. Alexander Hamilton first advocated the creation of a central national bank to help foster private banks and create a larger store of bank credit, which he believed would stimulate economic growth. This bank would also help carry out the financial responsibilities of Congress and the Department of the Treasury. The First National Bank of the United States was created in 1791, but its charter ran out twenty years later, throwing the American economy into turmoil. The Second National Bank, founded in 1816, was initially successful in regulating monetary regulation, but it was eventually deemed too powerful and a threat to democracy. Its dissolution in 1841 led to another period of chaos in which state-chartered banks struggled to regulate the monetary system.

Formation of the Federal Reserve System

In 1908, the United States established a National Monetary Commission to investigate the country's monetary policy. This group recommended the creation of a federal banking system, and the Federal Reserve Act became law in 1913, despite some critics who claimed that a central bank would place too much power in the hands of a small group.
The Federal Reserve Act created the Federal Reserve System to provide an elastic supply of currency, a way to give helpful credit to commercial interests to stimulate economic growth, and to be a supervisor for the nation's banks and financial institutions. After a long process of consultation with various business and government leaders, the Federal Reserve Bank, as it exists today, opened in 1914.

Federal Reserve System

The Federal Reserve System is the central bank in the United States, responsible for maintaining stable growth in the economy and creating monetary policy. The *Fed*, as it is called, does not deal with individual accounts; it is the bank for private banks and other depository institutions. The Fed also regulates and supervises banks, distributes currency to the public through the banks, facilitates the collection and transfer of checks, and implements some of the regulations of consumer credit legislation. The Federal Reserve System consists of the Board of Governors, the Federal Open Market Committee, twelve Federal Reserve Banks around the country, various branches of those Federal Reserve Banks, advisory committees, and some member financial institutions.

Highest Authority in the Federal Reserve System

The highest authority in the Federal Reserve System is the Board of Governors, which consists of seven members. These members, usually renowned economists, are appointed by the president and confirmed by the Senate, and serve terms of fourteen years. The main responsibility of the Board is to create and implement monetary policy, although it must also supervise the financial activity of banks, bank holding companies, and Federal Reserve System banks. The board decides how much money to loan these institutions and where to set the rate of interest on those loans. The Board also oversees any bank mergers and acquisitions for American banks, as well as those international banks that are members. The Board of Governors reports its activities to Congress.

Interstate Commerce Commission

The Interstate Commerce Commission (ICC) was established in 1887 by the Interstate Commerce Act. At first, it only regulated interstate commerce as it took place by rail or by a combination of water and rail. Now, it regulates railroads, trucks, buses, water carriers, and all the pipelines that are not overseen by the Federal Energy Regulatory Commission.
The ICC regulates the rates that carriers charge and oversees any mergers, acquisitions, and sales of carriers. Besides setting the rules for accounting, the ICC also grants the right to operate a railroad, trucking company, bus line, water carrier, or transportation broker. The ICC makes sure that the public receives the fair rates and reasonable service guaranteed by the Interstate Commerce Act. In this line, the ICC makes sure there is no discrimination, prejudice, or preferential treatment in the transportation industry.

National Debt, Deficits, and Surplus

A *national debt* is created when the federal government spends more money than it takes in. If the government is in debt, it must borrow money, and so the national debt includes not only the borrowed money but the interest that accrues on that money. To pay for this, the government issues treasury notes, bills, and bonds.
The national debt remains if it is not paid that year, and so over time a nation may have an *accumulated deficit* that is enormous. For instance, the United States had, in 1995, accumulated $4 trillion in debt since 1969.
The United States first began the policy of deficit spending during the Great Depression, in the hopes of stimulating the economy. *Deficit spending* occurs when a government spends more than it takes in through taxation.
A *surplus* is made when a government takes in more money than it spends.

Gross Domestic Product

The gross domestic product (GDP) of a country is the total value of goods and services produced by that country in a given period, usually a year. Measures of GDP are typically used to assess the growth of a nation's economy: A steadily increasing GDP indicates a healthy, expanding economy.
In the United States, GDP is calculated as the sum total of four components of aggregate demand: net exports (the total value of exports less the total value of imports); consumption (the total amount spent on durable goods, nondurable goods, and services); investment; and federal, state, and local government purchases. Mathematically, the equation for GDP looks like this:
GDP = consumption + investment + (government spending) + (exports − imports).
GDP is very similar to gross national product (GNP), except that GDP excludes net income from foreign sources.

Tax, Taxable Income, and Exemption

A *tax* is any payment demanded by the government to help pay for its operations. The federal government is largely funded by income tax, whereas the state government earns most of its money from property and sales taxes. The goal of the tax system is to be equitable both horizontally (people of the same income pay the same amount in taxes) and vertically (people pay an amount of taxes proportional to their income).

Taxable income is the amount of personal or corporate income that is left after all deductions, exemptions, and losses have been subtracted.

An *exemption* is an amount of money that, for some reason, is not eligible for taxation. Many individuals receive tax exemptions for the money they use to pay for dependents.

Itemized Deductions

The government generally allows individuals to avoid being taxed on certain expenses which, when they are listed and calculated on the individual's income tax form, are known as *itemized deductions*.

Medical and dental costs may be deductible if they are greater than 7.5% of income. Interest on a mortgage or on investments may be deductible. Items that are stolen or lost due to a natural disaster may be deductible as well. Other miscellaneous deductions may include the cost of work uniforms, job-search expenses, repayments of Social Security, some legal fees, home-office expenses, and educational expenses that are related to the individual's job. In the United States at this time, individuals cannot deduct political donations, raffle tickets, cosmetic surgery, life insurance, funeral expenses, gifts, tuition, home repairs, and commuting expenses, among other things.

Personal Taxation

Individuals may be subject to a number of taxes as they conduct their business in the United States. The greatest is the *income tax*, which is collected on both the federal and state levels and which is determined by the individual's level of income. The income tax is meant to be the tax that most clearly assesses the individual's ability to pay. Individuals may also be subject to a *property tax* based on buildings and land that they own. *Inheritance taxes* are assessed on any property an individual received upon the death of someone else. Individuals pay a *sales tax* in most states any time they purchase a good or a service. A *capital gains tax* is paid on the income received from the sale of capital assets, like stocks or bonds. *Social Security payments* are also a sort of tax levied on the individual, in which money is set aside to ensure the financial security of older workers.

Business Taxation

Corporations, because they are considered individual entities by the state, are required to pay *income tax* on their earnings. All other businesses are required to pay *property tax* on any buildings, land, or equipment that they own. Businesses also pay a regular *sales tax* on the goods and services that they purchase, and a *capital gains tax* on the monies made from the sale of capital assets, including securities and real estate. Businesses may be required to pay an *excise tax* if they sell certain goods, although the money for this tax is usually just added on to the price the ultimate consumer has to pay. Tobacco and gasoline are two products that carry an excise tax. A *value-added tax* is a tax that companies must pay on goods as they pass through the stages to becoming a finished product; companies are taxed according to the amount of value their work added to the product.

Management

Human Resource Accounting

Many business analysts believe human resources are more valuable than physical assets; some even go so far as to say that human resources should be listed as assets on the company's balance sheet. Most businesses spend a substantial amount of time recruiting and training their employees. Some analysts even say that, in the event of a recession, companies would do better to get rid of machinery or downsize inventory rather than fire trained employees. Oddly, though, human resources is one of the more neglected and undervalued areas of business. There is speculation that this is because effective human resource accounting requires a feel for employees that goes beyond objective charts and graphs.

Promotion from Within

One of the most important tasks of a business manager is the selection and training of new employees. "Promotion from within" is a straightforward concept, but besides indicating that a company tries to advance its own employees, it has come to refer more generally to the philosophy of establishing organizational loyalty. Many businesses claim to have a promotion-from-within policy because it is attractive to employees, though the company may do a considerable amount of external hiring. Sometimes the current employees of a company simply aren't appropriate candidates for management. Furthermore, if a new area of business opens up for a company, it will always make more sense to hire an external candidate who specializes in that area.

Managerial Control

In order to oversee business operations properly, managers must exercise effective control. Managerial control is simply making the adjustments that allow the business to be successful. The three essential steps of managerial control are the establishment of standards, the comparison of performance to those standards, and the actions taken to align performance with standards. Managerial standards should be explicit not only to management, but also to the staff. Furthermore, management should always make their assessment of performance at least somewhat transparent, so that employees can understand the criteria of judgment and remedy any mistakes they might be unconsciously making. Managers must react quickly to improve performance, but without interfering too much in day-to-day operations.

Common Problems in Organizational Management

There are a number of ways for the organization of a business to hinder operations. Some businesses have span of management problems, in which managers have too many immediate subordinates to be effective. On the other hand, if every manager has only a few subordinates, it is possible that the organization will have too many levels, will require more managers than necessary, and therefore will be needlessly expensive. Generally, managers can afford to have more direct subordinates if job assignments are clear, if the manager is a good communicator, and if the business is relatively stable. If subordinates are well trained and independent, it is possible to broaden the manager's span of control.

How Managers Motivate Employees

One of the most important jobs for a manager is to create an environment in which employees can operate at their maximum potential. This is perhaps a rebuttal to the stereotypical view of a manager as one who sits behind a desk all day doing paperwork. Managers try to ensure that all the members of their team are pulling in the same direction, and that, moreover, the goals of the company are clear and known. Managers must use their authority to create a situation in which employees will feel obliged to do their best. Of course, no manager has unlimited power; organizations typically rein in their managers by creating a set of company rules that govern how managerial authority may be expressed.

Ultimate Goal of All Managers

Every manager has surplus in mind as his or her ultimate goal. Businesses that create surpluses create profits, or the amount by which sales dollars exceed expense dollars. To achieve a surplus, managers must have a good idea of what their goals are, regardless of their position in the organization. They must treat management as both a science and an art. Management is a science insofar as it has certain reliable rules and can be studied in an organized fashion. Management is also an art insofar as it requires a degree of flexibility and intuition. Simply knowing the "rules of management" will not make someone an effective manager; such a person must also have intelligence, compassion, and an innate understanding of how to make teams work effectively.

Bias Toward Action and Benefits of Small Teams

Successful managers tend to have a bias toward action. This means that their immediate response to a problem is to act, rather than to sit and ponder the problem's cause. Well-managed companies quickly assess troubling situations and determine a proper course of action or reallocate resources as needed. If this course is unsuccessful, they have no qualms about changing course and trying something else. An effective manager will strive to avoid what is known as "paralysis by analysis."
Good managers will also try to keep their teams small, so that they can effectively oversee everyone and simplify communication and so that everyone on the team feels integral. Even large corporations try to keep their divisions small, so that every individual's job seems more important, and no one feels as if they are buried by bureaucracy.

Managerial Goals

Successful businesses are almost always driven by their customers; they make decisions based on the desires of the people to whom they sell their products. This means that companies do not make decisions based on technology or on production or on its overall strategy. All of these things are important, but they should be determined by the demands of the consumer.
Moreover, well-managed companies tend to emphasize improving productivity by means of helping employees become more effective rather than by improving technology. Good companies find that they can improve every aspect of their operation if they can motivate

and satisfy their employees. Employee satisfaction tends to positively influence many aspects of a business besides just basic productivity.

Managerial Practices that Encourage Entrepreneurship

Successful businesses will strive to create the opportunity for employees to conceive, develop, and implement profitable new ideas. To do so, managers cannot keep employees too tightly under their control. Entrepreneurship within a company will be encouraged if the management makes a point of rewarding successful innovations and employees feel they have the freedom to experiment in their work. Successful businesses will also try to emphasize a particular business value with almost religious zeal. If management transmits a consistent message to staff, there is less chance of confusion and chaos. Maintaining a constant set of goals ensures that all employees will know how best to perform their jobs.

Emphasis on Specialization and Loose–tight Controls

Although diversification seems to be a popular trend among large corporations, the businesses that are consistently successful are those that stick to the area of production with which they are most familiar. Some businesses may be more effective at new-product innovation, manufacturing, or marketing, and they should work to accentuate these strengths.
Another consistent feature of successful business is simultaneously loose and tight controls. This simply means that businesses should have fairly tight control on some things but still allow operating managers a great degree of freedom in others. Although top executives should always have a firm grasp on the overall workings of the business and its core values, it is best if they give their various divisional managers the freedom to operate within their individual areas of specialization.

Financial Analysis

Development and Use of Business Statistics

Most businesses rely on statistics to help them chart their past performance and determine the proper course of action for the future. In fact, one of the fastest-growing areas of the economy is the business analysis sector. Companies in this line of work collect information about a business and compare it with the published records of other businesses, to help their client determine how they shape up and how they can improve. The government also keeps extensive records of business statistics, for the purpose of making economic decisions. Increasingly, sophisticated software makes it possible for businesses to predict with a high degree of accuracy their productivity and general financial picture.

Basic Accounting Equation

The basic equation of accounting is that assets are equal to the sum of liabilities and capital (sometimes referred to as equity or proprietorship). This equation can be rearranged to show the total value of ownership: assets minus liabilities. Every transaction made by a business results in a change to one of these three categories. If the business borrows money from the bank, for instance, it increases its cash assets and its liabilities. If the business buys a new machine, it has increased its assets, but it has also decreased its cash assets or liabilities, depending on whether the machine was bought with cash or credit. When a business hires employees, its assets increase by whatever amount the new employee will produce, but the business has become liable for whatever it has agreed to pay the employee.

Property Rights in Accounting

All property entails certain rights and restrictions. When a person or a partnership owns a business, this ownership is registered as net worth, capital, or proprietorship. When a business has borrowed funds in order to sustain operations, the claims of their lenders are known as liabilities. Businesses may also have a liability to their employees, insofar as they must pay their employees at regular intervals. Taxes on property are also considered a liability. In the case of the corporation, property ownership and rights are a bit more complicated. Since the corporation functions as an independent entity, it has its own rights and responsibilities. Still, stockholders own the corporation, though they do not personally assume its liabilities. They instead have what is called stockholders' equity, the amount of their original investment plus accumulated profits not paid out in dividends.

Accounts Receivable and Accounts Payable

The phrases accounts receivable and accounts payable refer to transactions in which payment is delayed. When a business sells a product to someone today but will not be paid for another thirty days, the amount that the buyer owes is considered an account receivable. Assuming that the increase in accounts receivable is more than the product was worth as an asset in its own right, the business has made a profit, or an increase in capital or proprietorship. On the other hand, businesses may buy materials and agree to pay for them later. Until they are paid for, the materials increase the firm's assets (in this case, the business inventory) and liabilities. Such liabilities are called accounts payable.

Debits and Credits

In accounting, any transaction that increases the assets of a firm or reduces its liabilities or proprietorship is called a debit. Any transaction that decreases assets or increases liabilities or proprietorship is known as a credit. Every business transaction will affect at least two accounts, one being a debit and the other being a credit of an equal amount. One of the main ways that accountants check their books for errors is by adding up all the debits and credits and making sure that the two numbers are equal. Though these terms are often a source of confusion for beginning accounting students, they are really quite easy to use if one simply bears in mind that a credit (or "addition") to a liability account means the business has lost value, and a debit to liabilities means that the business gains value; in other words, the crediting and debiting applies only to the specific account, and not to the business as a whole.

Balance in Detail

Every business transaction has a cost and a value; when material is purchased, for instance, physical assets are increased and either assets (cash) or liabilities (credit) are increased. For this reason, accountants use what is known as double-entry bookkeeping, a system of records wherein every transaction provides a total number of debits equal to the total number of credits. Occasionally, a business may have more liabilities than it has assets, resulting in a decrease in the claims of the ownership. However, if the business' liabilities exceed its net worth, then the business is technically insolvent. If the business can sell enough of its assets to satisfy the immediate claims of creditors and continue operations, it is known as a deficit.

Actual Costs and Actual Sales

One important thing to remember about accounting is that it is always based on actual costs and sales rather than any other measures. For example, if a business purchases some land for a certain amount, and the land then doubles in value, the firm still considers the land as having the original value when it performs its accounting. The only adjustment to such an asset is depreciation, the expression of the loss of value due to the wearing out of an asset (for instance a machine, which becomes less valuable from year to year). Similarly, a business always registers its actual sales in its accounting documents: even if a product is normally sold at a higher price, the form will only account for the money made in the particular sale at the particular sale price.

Problems Inflation Cause in Accounting

Inflation can cause major problems for accountants, since it can make it impossible for them to accurately predict costs. For instance, a business may assume that it can purchase the same amount of materials at the same price from year to year, but any inflation will make this impossible. This change in price value can make accounting reports quite misleading; some companies, for instance, will report excellent profits that, once inflation is taken into account, turn out to be poor or mediocre. The United States government has tried to remedy this problem by forcing large companies to report the effects of price inflation on accounts to their stockholders. Nevertheless, this is still no better than a crude solution to a very difficult problem.

Balance Sheet

Double-entry bookkeeping appears on what is known as a balance sheet: an accounting statement that describes the relationship between assets, which are indicated on the left side of the sheet, and the claims against those assets made by creditors or owners, indicated on the right. Balance sheets may be quite simple, as in the case of small businesses, or very complex, as for large corporations. Some businesses must use what is known as a consolidated balance sheet to combine their accounts with the accounts of the other companies in which that business has a significant interest. For large corporations, the balance sheet offers an opportunity for stockholders to view the raw data of the business, and to interpret its progress.

Items on a Balance Sheet

Some of the items commonly found on a balance sheet may require a bit of explanation. For instance, the item called "time deposits and marketable securities" refers to money that has been deposited in a bank and is earning interest, as well as investments in government bonds, stocks, or other securities that can be easily exchanged. Timed deposits and marketable securities are added to cash to find the total of assets equivalent to cash. The item "prepaid expenses" refers to rent and insurance premiums that have already been paid. "Accrued income and other taxes" refers to taxes on income that are owed to the federal government, state governments, and foreign governments. Generally, these taxes must be paid early in the following year.

Interpretation of Assets on a Balance Sheet

There are a few important observations to make when assessing a business' balance sheet. First, take a look at cash: it may be stable or rising, but it also may include a rise in short-term borrowings and accounts payable, which could be worrisome to an investor. The item "accounts and notes receivable" will indicate the progress of sales, as lower sales typically require fewer receivables (goods that are sold, but for which the business has yet to be paid). A balance sheet might also include categories under assets like "construction in progress," indicating that the business is making some kind of transition. One might also want to consider the accountant's estimation of depreciation, to determine whether the business' assets hold the value he or she claims.

Interpretation of Liabilities and Equity

When assessing a business' liabilities on a balance sheet, there are several key areas to check. First, a rise in short-term liabilities might indicate that the business has recently had to borrow a great deal of money to finance some expansion project. If short-term borrowings are low for a large business, investors can be assured that the business still has the potential to borrow considerable money against accounts receivable should it be necessary. The long-term liabilities indicated on a balance sheet are also important; even if assets clearly cover any liabilities, the interest accrued on long-term debts can damage finances. The figures listed under stockholder's equity indicate when and how many dividends have been paid. Treasury stock is any stock in the corporation that was sold to the public and then repurchased by the corporation; it has the potential to be sold again.

Income Statement

Although the balance sheet is very helpful in assessing the financial status of a business, it cannot indicate exactly what happened during a given year, what sales and expenses were, and what the exact profit was. For this information, accountants use an income statement. The income statement describes in summary form the sales for some period of time (a month, three months, or a year, typically). It then subtracts the expenses incurred by that business during the same period, and gives the resulting amount as either a profit or a loss. For this reason, most people consider the income statement to be the clearest indicator of a business' fortunes. Of course, every business must begin to turn a profit at some point if it aims to continue operating.

Sales, Net Sales, and Cost of Goods Sold

A normal income statement combines several distinct categories. Sales are considered to be the total amount of goods or services that a business has sold in the period. Sales are considered final when the item or service is delivered, even if it has not yet been paid for. Net sales are simply sales less returned merchandise, discounts granted for prompt payment, and reductions in cost for damaged goods. The cost of goods sold, also called the cost of production, is the amount that it took to produce all the goods that were sold. It typically includes the cost of the materials needed to create the goods, the cost of the labor used to make the good, and the overhead costs (electricity, machine maintenance, etc.) associated with making that good.

Gross Profit, Operating Expenses, and Income from Operations

The standard income statement has a number of different categories. Gross profit is calculated as the net sales minus the cost of the goods sold (also called the cost of production). The operating expenses for a business are any expenses that are not directly related to the production of a good or performance of a service. Some examples of operating expenses are rent, utilities, insurance, depreciation on buildings, and managerial salaries. Income from operations is calculated as gross profit minus operating expenses. This is the company's profit before adjusting for interest payments, income, or expenses that are not directly related to the business (for instance, royalties on patents, income from investments, losses from unpaid sales). It is also the income before income taxes.

Income Before Income Taxes, Income Taxes, and Net Income

Once sales and expenses have been fully tabulated, the income statement gives a summary of income. Income before income taxes is the profit the company has made, after adjusting for miscellaneous expenses or income. Because interest expenses are deducted from the total at this point, income before income taxes is usually less than income from operations. Income taxes, of course, are the taxes the business owes to various agencies of the government for the income earned during that particular period. Net income, otherwise known as profit, is the final yield of the business after all expenses and taxes have been considered. This is the amount available to pay stockholders in the form of dividends, or to reinvest in the business. A negative amount here represents a loss.

Tracking Cash in a Business

For most companies, having available cash is even more important than turning a profit. A company that takes a loss need not suspend operations as long as it has a ready supply of cash. In the opposite way, a business may appear to be quite profitable and yet flounder if it does not have access to cash. For this reason, it is important to get a sense of how much cash a business has available by looking at its balance sheet. If all the assets of the business are represented by machinery and real estate, for instance, the business has a problem. Employees, after all, cannot be paid in machinery! In order to fully assess a business, one must analyze how much cash it has, as well as how much it is likely to be able to borrow if necessary.

Generation of Cash

Some businesses are better at generating and holding onto cash. If a business has vast expenses payable in cash, it had better be bringing in a lot of cash to offset these expenses. Assuming the business does not invest in other ways, profits generally mean an increase in cash. Cash can also be brought into a business by loans from ownership. An increase in accounts payable is much the same as borrowing cash, because the business gets the materials it needs without losing the use of the cash owed for them. Similarly, reducing accounts receivable means increasing cash, as prior customers have finally paid off their purchases. Any large expenditures typically require a reduction in cash, as will a reduction in accounts payable. Reduction of inventory typically means an increase in cash, as products have been sold.

Access to Financial Status

For obvious reasons, a number of people may need to assess the financial status of a business. These people may be investors in the business, people who have lent the business money and want to be paid back, or the managers of the business itself. One of the most common ways to judge a balance sheet quickly is to perform a ratio analysis. A ratio analysis measures the relationship between two different items, for instance assets and liabilities. Analysts use various ratios to see how businesses compare to one another. Usually, a business will be compared only with other businesses in the same industry, but one of the advantages of ratio analysis is that it allows businesses of widely differing size and structure to be easily compared.

Current Ratio

The current ratio is one of the most common measurements used to analyze a balance sheet. It is the ratio of current assets to current liabilities. This measure is very important to lenders, and so it is often used by banks and other businesses that allow the business being considered to buy on credit. Typically, lenders are encouraged when a business has twice as many assets as liabilities. This ratio indicates that the business will have no trouble meeting its liabilities, even if its current assets shrink due to an inability to collect accounts receivable or because of a loss of inventory. Current liabilities, of course, will remain constant. The safe amount of assets for a particular business may depend on the form of those assets: assets in the form of machinery are much more difficult to exchange to pay off liabilities.

Acid Test Ratio and Debt to Net Worth Ratio

The acid test ratio, also known as the quick ratio, is the ratio of cash and accounts receivable to current liabilities. This ratio excludes inventory, and only includes those assets that can be quickly converted into cash to meet current liabilities. Generally, an acceptable standard for this ratio is one to one. The debt to net worth ratio is the ratio of the total debt to the equity of the stockholders. This is essentially a measure of the money put into the company by the owners compared with the money put into the company by lenders. From the perspective of banks it is healthy for businesses to have debts equal to no more than half of the ownership equity. If the company is especially profitable, however, banks may not be concerned as long as debt is equal to net worth.

Collection Period of Accounts Receivable

Analysts should be able to look at the balance sheet for a business and determine whether the amount of accounts receivable is cause for worry. They can do this by calculating the number of days of sales represented by the accounts receivable. The calculation is done by dividing the sales figure by the value of accounts receivable, to derive the number of times accounts will turn over in a year. This figure is then converted into days to determine the number of days of sales represented by accounts receivable, a total known as the collection period. In most manufacturing businesses, the collection period ranges from 35 to 55 days. If it extends much beyond that, analysts will be concerned that many of these accounts will be uncollectible; if it is much shorter, a strict credit policy may be driving off potential business.

Gross Profit Margin

The gross profit margin is one of the measures taken to analyze the income statements of a company. It is a ratio indicating the percentage that gross profit (deducting cost of services or products but not deducting operating expenses, taxes, and other items) bears to total sales. Essentially, it is the amount that the business has available to pay for whatever expenses are not directly related to the production of a service or product. Most successful manufacturing firms have gross profit margins of about 25 to 35 percent. This is considered to be the most effective way of comparing businesses in the same industry. If a business cannot make a gross profit equal to or better than the industry standard, it is not likely to last for very long.

Use of Pretax Profit Margin

Analysts use the pretax profit margin to assess a business' income statement. The pretax profit margin is the business' profits before taxes as a percentage of sales. This ratio is widely considered to be the true measure of the profitability of a company, because it measures the percentage of each sales dollar that is registered as profits before taxes. Manufacturing firms usually have around eight to ten percent of the sales dollar as their pretax profit margin. Of course, businesses that have a large volume of sales in relation to the amount of investment will typically have lower pretax profit margins. Supermarkets, for instance, which turn their inventory over constantly, have pretax profit margins between one and two percent.

Measures of Profitability

Financial analysts can measure the profitability of a business by looking at the amount earned after income taxes. This information is found on the company's income statement. Of course, the standards for this measure will vary from company to company, depending on the special tax restrictions. Typically, income taxes amount to about half of net income before taxes, so the percentage of net income to sales after taxes is usually half that of pretax income to sales. In other words, income taxes take about half of the money that a business makes in sales. The percentage of profit after taxes to sales for manufacturing businesses is generally around five percent. The ratio of profit after taxes to net worth assesses what the owners of a company are making from their investment. It is calculated by taking the profits after taxes and dividing them by the net worth of the business.

General Ledger

A general ledger, also known as a nominal ledger, is the central record of accounts for a business that uses double-entry bookkeeping. A general ledger usually includes accounts for fixed assets; current assets; liabilities; profits or losses; income and expenditure; and reserves. The general ledger is essentially a summary of all the financial activity of the company. It takes its data from the general journal, where all of the business transactions are recorded. A proper general ledger should make it possible for the business to see the effects of any transaction on the company's entire financial outlook. Besides just the numerical data for each transaction, the general ledger includes the date and a brief description of the transaction.

Calculating Depreciation of Equipment and Other Assets

Calculating depreciation of equipment is one of the biggest challenges to accuracy in accounting. Depreciation may be classified as general wearing down of equipment, obsolescence, or predictable mechanical failures. It is important to assess depreciation accurately, because otherwise assets may be overstated. There are several theories of how to calculate depreciation. The simplest means is straight-line depreciation, in which the company determines how much the equipment may be sold for at some future date and then assumes it will lose equal amounts of value every year until it reaches that price. Declining-balance depreciation is a slightly more sophisticated method: it operates on the assumption that an asset will decline in value most in its first few years of operation. Activity methods of measuring depreciation consider not the length of ownership, but how often the item is used

Calculation of the Cost of Goods Sold

The cost of goods sold is all of the expenses directly related to producing a particular good for sale. This can include the cost of the materials, as well as the labor needed to make the good. The cost of goods sold does not include things like office expenses, shipping, or advertising. The cost of goods sold can be determined by combining all of the costs associated with the creation of a particular good, and then dividing this total by the number of those goods that are sold. The gross profit on that good is then determined by subtracting the cost of goods sold from the sales revenue generated by that good. In order to determine net profit, however, a business also has to subtract all of the indirect expenses that are incurred during operation.

Trial Balance

In accounting, a trial balance is the worksheet on which all of the balances from the various ledgers are entered into two columns: debit and credit. Trial balances are typically prepared during each financial period, in summation of the closing of the previous ledgers. Accuracy is indicated by whether the total of the debit side is equal to the total of the credit side. Basically, the trial balance is used to pinpoint any errors that have been made during the creation of the ledger. It should be noted, though, that an accurate trial balance does not necessarily indicate an accurate ledger; for example, if a debit and credit are switched by accident, this will not unbalance the ledger, though it will present false data.

Worksheets

A worksheet is an accounting form used to combine all of the information from various ledgers on one sheet of paper. Worksheets typically have either six or eight columns, depending on how much information the business feels obliged to list. A standard six-column worksheet has a list of the business' accounts (that is, the various other firms and individuals that the business has had transactions with, as well as the various incomes and expenses the business has incurred) on the left, and then there are columns where the data from the trial balance, income statement, and balance sheet is entered. Once all of the account information has been entered, the net income can be calculated by adding together all the debits and all the credits, and finding the difference.

Reasons for Inaccuracy in Traditional Accounting

Though accounting strives to provide an accurate view of the financial status of a business, there are several reasons why its calculations may miss the mark. For one thing, assets often change their value while a business owns them: machines may become obsolete, or land may increase in value. Measuring the depreciation of assets is an inexact science. Some firms carry a great deal of inventory, and it is difficult to say whether this inventory is worth what the accounting records suggest, because it is impossible to predict whether it will ever be sold, and at what price. Finally, it is very difficult to allocate the costs that will be incurred by a large business. While it is easy to see how much labor and machinery equals a certain amount of product, it is more difficult to say how much insurance or executive salary will equal that same amount of product.

Primary Reason for Accounting

Every business owns property, and this property comes with certain rights: therefore, business accounting is necessary. The operations of the business cause changes in the amount and kind of property owned by the business, and the changes can be expressed in terms of dollars and cents. The property owned by a business may be any number of things: for instance, manufacturing firms own equipment, land, and buildings, and law firms own books, offices, and office equipment. Every business requires a certain amount of cash to pay the bills. All of this property is considered the assets of the business. Every business, no matter how large or small, will need assets in order to operate.

Customer Relations

Telephone Etiquette and Customer Complaints

Since an individual's first contact with a business may be over the phone, it is essential that employees are schooled in proper telephone etiquette. When an employee (a receptionist, for example) answers the phone for someone else, he should always identify himself and the company he represents. Then, he should always ask how the other person can be helped. It is important not to make commitments on behalf of other people; it is better to promise to pass on a message rather than to say that a superior will call back at a particular time. Finally, it is very important to always take accurate and legible messages that include the time, date, reason for the call, degree of urgency, company represented by the caller, and any other relevant information.

Desired Voice and Image

There are some general strategies that students can use to immediately improve their telephone manner. As far as one's voice, one should always strive for clarity, so that every word can be understood. One should also try to cultivate warmth, naturalness, and expressiveness. Many writers on the subject recommend adopting a lower, mellower vocal pitch; they claim that this style of speech is more soothing to customers. In order to create a good image on the phone, employees should avoid using slang or chewing gum. They should never slam the phone down or fail to introduce themselves and offer a few courteous words. Last, and perhaps most important, employees should always keep the promises they make on the telephone.

Types of Customers

Although most people think of private citizens when they envision the American consumer, marketing executives must consider a few other customer profiles when they plan their strategies. Industrial buyers are those that purchase goods with the intent to resell them, either as is or in an altered form. Most complex products (books, for instance) are the result of many industrial sales. Commercial buyers are those that don't alter goods before resale. They include hotels, offices, banks, schools, hospitals, and theaters. The things they buy may be used in production, or resold without any change. Governments, perhaps surprisingly to some, are the largest consumers in the United States. They buy everything from office supplies to nuclear warheads.

Entrepreneurship and Business Organizations

Entrepreneurship

Entrepreneurship is the process of collecting and organizing the financial, technological, and managerial resources necessary to start a new business venture with the aim of making a profit. Entrepreneurship is considered to be the foundation of the free market economy, as it rewards hard work and innovation.

Advocates of free market capitalism suggest that the process of entrepreneurship benefits both the entrepreneur and the society as a whole: the former by the chance for great material gain, and the latter by the creative and diverse product market that is created as a result of it. Although entrepreneurship is typically thought of as an activity of lone, self-interested individuals, some economists argue that the characteristics of innovation and risk-taking can also be found in dynamic corporations.

Basic Organizational Structure of a Business

Any business organization of a decent size will have a division of labor, a structure for making decisions, and some formal rules and policies. A typical vertical division of labor has three levels: top executives, middle managers, and low managers and laborers. The horizontal division of labor is the division of each level into groups with a specific and unique purpose.

There are several basic business organizational structures. *Functional* is organized around job functions, *product* is organized around the various products sold, *matrix* is a combination of functional and product organizational structures, and *territorial* is organized around the various regions in which the company has units.

Decision-making structures of business organizations vary, depending on whether the top executives make all important calls or if authority is delegated. The *delegation of authority* is the process through which managers give the authority to make decisions or to take action to other individuals or groups under their control. Rules and regulations may be either formal or informal, depending on whether they are written and known to all, are crucial in maintaining efficiency in a business.

Kinds of Business Structure

Successful businesses always select the organizational business model, or structure, that best fits their needs. There are several structures by which businesses are organized.

A *functional structure* divides the parts of the business up by what they do, or the functions they perform. Possible divisions in such an organization might be production, accounting, marketing, and so on.

A *territorial structure* is typical of businesses whose operations are spread out across a series of locations; it just makes sense to have each location operate somewhat independently.

Some large companies have what is known as a *product structure*, in which divisions are made among the parts of the business that sell different products. An auto manufacturer, for instance, might have different divisions for cars and trucks.

A *matrix structure* combines functional and product structures, thus arranging for both financial and production managers to oversee a given project. For example, an accounting manager and a marketing manager, among others, would each oversee the managers of each independent product line.

Line and Staff Organization Structures

The chains of command in a business organization follow either the line or staff organization structure.

In a *line organization*, the chain of command runs from a top executive to his subordinate executives, from the subordinate executives to their own subordinates, and so on down the line. In addition, All employees consult only with their immediate superior.

In a *line and staff structure*, however, that line of command remains, but individuals are also advised by other departments depending on the project. Most large businesses use a line and staff structure, so that responsibility to one's immediate boss is emphasized without removing the potentially beneficial advice provided by other superiors. Executives will often give functional authority over their subordinates to department heads who are knowledgeable about the current project.

Centralization and Decentralization of Authority

A business organization is centralized when there is little delegation of authority, and decisions are mostly made by the top executives. Obviously, the most extreme version of centralization is when one owner makes all the decisions in a business. Decentralization, conversely, is exhibited in a business where authority is dispersed widely throughout. Most businesses operate in degrees of centralization and decentralization. Important decisions, particularly those regarding large amounts of capital, are usually reserved for top executives, while more routine decisions are likely made by lower managers. Business analysts have noted that most businesses tend to be too centralized in their early years but can become too decentralized once they have had some success and established a company policy.

Organizational Planning

It is extremely important for business managers to adjust their firm's organizational structure to suit changes in the business and to anticipate what adjustments will need to be made in the future. Organization is essentially a setting in which employees can perform; as the needs of the business and the demands of the market change over time, the setting appropriate to maximizing employee performance will also change.

It is also important that roles in a business be clearly defined and that the leaders of the business envision what roles will be needed in the future. It is impossible to recruit or train the appropriate workers without having a vision of what the firm's needs will be. Most businesses will discover that, as they grow over time, their organizational structure will become more and more complex.

Budgeting System of a Business

A budget is a formal document that describes the financial history of a business and projects the expenses, income, credits, and debits for an upcoming period, typically a year. A complete budgeting process entails planning long-term goals, assigning the budgeting process to a specific group of trained individuals, organizing information from every area of the business, directing authority so that managers at every level assist with the process, and controlling future activity to make sure that it is in line with the approved budget. Successful budgeting enhances the ability of managers to see long-term goals, alerts the business to potential problems, coordinates the various activities of the business, evaluates the ongoing performance of the various divisions, and shapes the accounting department's overall view of company history.

Benevolent-Authoritative Style of Management

The benevolent-authoritative style of management is one in which there is a clear distinction between management and labor, although unlike that used in the exploitative-authoritative model. In a benevolent-authoritative system, the assumption is that management acts in the best interest of the workers.

In this model, managers have a great deal of responsibility and workers have very little, and there is almost no communication between the various levels of the company hierarchy, and very little cooperation between the different levels of the business. Managers tend to adopt a patronizing attitude toward their employees and may frequently fail to understand and take into account their employees' feelings. The benevolent-authoritative model is much more common and unremarkable than the exploitative-authoritative model of management, but it, too, is considered to be ineffective.

Consultative Style of Management

In the consultative style of management, leaders place a small degree of trust in their employees, but they still do not allow workers an equal voice in the operations of the company. In this model of management, employees are motivated by potential rewards for productivity, and there is some quality interaction between the various levels of the business hierarchy.

More than in the authoritative models, employees may feel some responsibility for the success of the business, and there may be a degree of teamwork between the various groups. In this model, because managers trust their subordinates somewhat, they give them freedom to act on a host of minor issues. Still, ultimate responsibility is in the hands of management, and so lower-level employees are not trusted with very important matters.

Participative-Group Style of Management

The participative-group style of management is considered, by most analysts, to be the most effective means of leading a business. In this model, managers have absolute trust in their subordinates because they have ensured that every employee is properly trained and competent.

Employees in this kind of business will be motivated by rewards rather than punishment, and they will have a clear idea of the company's objectives. There will be a large degree of cooperation and communication among the various levels of the business, and all employees will feel that their work directly affects the success of the company. According to business analysts, this model results in the most profitable businesses with the most satisfied and productive employees.

Sole Proprietorships

A *sole proprietorship* is any business that is completely owned by one person and has no separate existence from that person. Sole proprietorships are relatively easy to open: the individual only needs to obtain the relevant licenses. This is the most common form of business. Sole proprietorships are attractive to many entrepreneurs because they offer the opportunity for total control, as well as the flexibility in decision-making afforded by what is usually a one-person management team.

Sole proprietorships are often run under the owner's social security number, unless the company has employees, and all liabilities are the owner's.

Such businesses need much less government supervision and licensing and are, therefore, less expensive to start. On the other hand, sole proprietorships frequently suffer from a limited source of capital, and the risk for the owner is often great. The success of the business is also dependent on the health of one person, making any illness or infirmity potentially devastating.

Advantages of Sole Proprietorship

The owner of a sole proprietorship has the most concentrated control of any business person. He or she is not required to share plans, policies, or methods of operation with anyone else. Because the owner has the sole right to all profits, he or she is likely to be more motivated to succeed than the employee of a corporation or partnership. It is also extremely easy to start up or dissolve a sole proprietorship. There is no need for a contract as in partnerships, or incorporation papers as in corporations. The owner is subject only to the relevant government regulations. Unlike the corporation, the proprietorship does not have to pay income taxes on its profits. Instead, the owner must simply pay the taxes on his personal income.

Disadvantages of Sole Proprietorship

There are some disadvantages to running a sole proprietorship. For one thing, it is often difficult for a single individual to assemble the capital necessary to start a business. Whatever start-up investment is going to be made is limited to the resources of the proprietor.

There is also a great deal of personal risk in a sole proprietorship because the proprietor is responsible for all the losses incurred by the business. Also, it is quite common for the personal assets of the proprietor to be combined with the assets of the business, so getting in trouble with creditors can result in the loss of personal property.

It can also be difficult to attract top managers to a proprietorship because they will desire some financial ownership. The ease with which sole proprietorships can be formed and dissolved means that they will often start without adequate planning and are, therefore, more likely to fail.

Corporation

A *corporation* is a company or group that has been granted, by the government, the rights of a distinct and viable entity. Ownership of a corporation is held by individuals who own shares of the corporation's stock.

One of the main advantages of the corporation is that individual shareholders are not responsible for its actions; they can only lose their initial investment. Indeed, employees of the corporation cannot be prosecuted for the acts of the corporation at large. Many critics say that this system of corporate rights has led to some immoral business practices. In any case, large corporations have enormous influence in the modern global economy: they can attract the best managers, manipulate government policy to suit their ends, and in many ways become national economies in their own right.

Corporate Governance

Corporate governance refers to the rules and regulations under which a business operates. It is the system that defines authority within the business and also accountability both within the business and externally to governments and investors.
In a corporation, stockholders elect the members of a board of directors to oversee the operations of the corporation. Typically, one share of stock amounts to one vote in a corporation election. In this system, a few major stockholders may hold sway over much larger groups of small shareholders. However, real power is usually held not by the stockholders but by the management group, who often cooperate with a few major stockholders to ensure that they remain in power. This arrangement is frequently aided by proxies, the permission given by stockholders to someone else to manage the stockholder's interest in the corporation. Oftentimes, corporate officers cultivate these proxies to maintain their position.

Advantages of a Corporation

The owners of a corporation—the stockholders—have only a limited liability over the fortunes of the business, and so they do not stand to incur devastating losses. Because the corporation is considered a legal entity, it is responsible for its own debts. This limited risk makes it easier for corporations to attract investment. The vastness of most corporate structures makes it possible for them to place authority in the hands of the most qualified individuals and to develop specialized job roles so that, in theory, everyone does the task for which they are best suited. Ownership of corporations is easily transferable, and the transfer of ownership rarely has any effect on the daily operations of the business. For these reasons, corporations tend to have longer and more stable histories than other forms of business.

Disadvantages of a Corporation

One disadvantage of the corporate form is that it results in double taxation: the corporation is taxed as a legal entity, and shareholders must pay income taxes on their dividends. Furthermore, these individual stockholders are unlikely to have any real control over the business, and so they may feel powerless to make needed changes.
Incorporation can be difficult and time-consuming, and corporations can face difficulties in organization and management because of their size, a problem that smaller proprietorships and partnerships avoid. Also, corporations are required to make regular reports to their shareholders, and so they cannot preserve too many secrets about their operations. Also, there is always the danger of low motivation among corporate employees because managers may not have much direct interest in the long-term success of the business.

Partnerships and Joint Ventures

A *partnership* is a business that is operated by two or more principals for the purpose of making a profit. It can also be a legal contract agreed to by two or more parties, in which they agree to jointly provide capital and labor for some enterprise in exchange for a determined proportion of profits or losses.

A *limited partnership* is any business partnership in which the responsibilities and the liabilities of one party are restricted to some degree, usually to the amount of that party's investment.

A *joint venture* is any business enterprise in which the parties share responsibility and benefits to a predetermined degree. The parties are bound together until the conditions listed in the original agreement are met to the satisfaction of all.

Advantages of a Partnership

Partnerships have many of the same advantages as sole proprietorships. There is a great amount of control concentrated in the partners, and their motivation to succeed is likely to be very high. Partnerships are a good chance for individuals with different sets of skills to team up. No government permission is required for a partnership, and business affairs do not need to be shared outside the partnership. Partnerships are easy to form and dissolve, and it may be easier for two people to raise sufficient start-up capital than it would be for a single individual. Also, the partnership, as a business form, is not required to pay income taxes, whereas the corporation must. Most partnerships are less heavily taxed than individuals in a corporation.

Disadvantages of a Partnership

The most serious disadvantage of the partnership is the high liability for losses assumed by the members. Moreover, any general partner in a partnership has the ability to bind the business to contracts and other obligations, making it a risky form of business in which to participate. Partnerships can also be very unstable. Any injury or illness to one partner may seriously hinder the business or force it to seek a new ownership arrangement. Even worse, if one partner is discovered to be incompetent, it is extremely difficult to force that person out of the partnership. Deciding on appropriate compensation for an unwanted partner can amount to long court battles and crippling legal fees. Many members of a partnership wishing to exit the agreement have a very hard time finding people to take their place.

Examples of a Cooperative

A *cooperative* is a group of individuals or smaller groups that join together to achieve some common goals. Cooperatives are often formed by minority interests who want to improve their power in the market. An example of this kind of cooperative is a farm collective, in which small farmers band together in an effort to get better prices and a bigger market for their crops. The cooperative model has also extended into credit unions, retail consumer groups, residential organizations, and marketing associations. Many retail cooperatives offer their members the chance to receive a significant discount in exchange for working in the store. The cooperative model is praised for giving the worker a clear stake in the results of his or her labor, as well as returning some market power to smaller interests.

Board of Directors

A *board of directors* is the group that is elected by the shareholders of a corporation to oversee the business. The board of directors selects upper-level management, including the chief executive officer (CEO), and supervises the strategic and financial objectives. Theoretically, all of this is meant to be done in the best interests of the shareholders. A typical model has the board of directors subdivided into committees dealing with nominating future members of the board, determining executive compensation, overseeing internal audits, and supervising financial operations. Many members of a board of directors will be senior executives at other companies. In recent years, some have criticized corporate boards for mindlessly following the whims of a popular CEO.

The Purpose of Managers

Managers are the people responsible for the performance of one or more people below them in the hierarchy of a business. Businesses that have only one employee can do without managers, but any business larger than one or two people will eventually require some leadership in the form of management. As businesses grow and become more complex, it becomes necessary to create more layers of management to oversee all the aspects of the business. In some very large companies, there can be up to ten or twelve layers of management. If they are functioning effectively, business managers are catalysts—agents that make a business work more effectively. However, in order to do this, a manager must know his or her job, must be an excellent communicator, and must have excellent judgment.

Important Elements in a Business Environment

Managers need to keep a few key things in mind when developing a proper business environment. It is essential that every position have a defined set of goals, and business plans and objectives must be fully understood by every member of the team. To achieve this standard, the manager must ensure that all the roles in the company are clearly defined. Furthermore, managers should try to remove any obstacles that may be preventing the business from reaching these goals. These could be money obstacles, which can be altered, or legal restrictions, which cannot.
The manager must also keep in mind the motivations of his or her employees and know how to entice them to do their best work. Finally, managers should consider how best to tailor the workplace to take best advantage of the natural strengths of the employees.

Business Planning

Business managers engage in business planning when they envision a desired future for the business and define strategies for reaching that future. Productive planning will honestly assess the current status of the business, anticipate trends in the market, and consider the financial implications of proposed plans. It should follow the scientific methods of observation and experiment and include every aspect of the business.
Planning is impossible without good records from the accounting department and cooperation from every division of the business. Out of the planning process, a management team should arrive at a set of long-term goals that will be the aims of short-term budgeting decisions. Ideally, coherent business plans allow every member of the company to understand the long-term goals of the business and contribute toward the realization of those goals.

Business Objectives and Policies

Business objectives are the goals to which the business is aiming. For a business to be successful, its objectives must be clear and attainable. Those objectives must also be verifiable; it is much less motivating to ask employees to do their best than it is to set a specific production goal.

Business policies, on the other hand, are statements of purpose that will define the way a business goes about achieving its goals. The managers of a business must have certain rules to guide them in making decisions; company policy provides that guidance. A successful set of policies, however, will not only set limits to business activity but also encourage initiative. Setting policy is a way for the founders of a business to stay in control without directly overseeing every aspect of that business. Policies must be regularly revised if they are to remain relevant.

Business Strategies and Procedures

Business strategies are the overall plans that are built around such external factors as trends in the marketplace or the actions of competitors. Strategy is determined by what kind of company the managers want to create. It implies a certain course of action and, as such, implies a commitment of human resources and capital..A strategy does not bother with small-scale plans but rather creates a loose framework of objectives for the company. Business procedures, however, must be very clear. Procedures specify exactly how future actions should be performed. Business managers often publish extensive lists of business procedures in the hopes of ensuring that employees will perform properly even when the managers are not around. There is always the danger that procedures will become so complicated and extensive that they will ultimately undermine their intention to aid productivity.

Business Rules and Programs

Business rules are things that employees are either required or forbidden to do. Rules are, in a sense, similar to procedures and plans in that they control future action. Procedures might even be considered sequences of rules. Rules are very necessary, but too often, they are conceived simply to prevent anyone from making a mistake. Some rules can discourage innovation. Managers should often consider what might be a more effective means of suggestion: making something a guideline or a rule. Business programs are the combinations of goals, policies, procedures, rules, job assignments, and resources that are necessary to carry out a certain plan of action. Business programs must be clearly supported by a budget that covers operating expenses and capital expenditures.

First Step of The Business Planning Process

The first step of business planning is to become aware of an opportunity to capitalize on. Once an opportunity is discovered, business managers should undertake an analysis of it to determine the best way to proceed. This analysis should move in several directions as managers must consider the potential market, the actions of competitors, and the strengths and weaknesses of their business. The company should also consider practical matters like how long the proposed process will take and how much it is likely to cost. All of these questions are essential if a business is to set goals that are appropriate and attainable; every company has limits to its resources and capital, and managers would do well to appreciate the limitations of their business before setting any goals.

Second Step of the Business Planning Process

For a business plan to be viable, its proposed course of action must have a clear and verifiable objective. Once the business has determined and considered an opportunity in the market, the next step is to set its goals. Of course, profit is the general goal in almost all businesses, but there must be more concrete production and distribution goals if a business is to proceed knowledgeably. A business may establish tapping into a new market as a goal, even if that new market does not immediately provide financial benefits. Large objectives may be supported by smaller objectives, like making a certain amount of money in one division or increasing productivity in another. These objectives are the goals for all of the plans that the business will soon be constructing.

Third Step of the Business Planning Process

After noting an opportunity and setting objectives, a business must begin to envision the necessary environment in which the objectives can be met. In other words, managers must develop the premises of their future plans. This might entail forecasting changes in the market, assessing population growth, or anticipating changes in the price level. Envisioning these premises also means considering which resources the company will need to use to bring a plan to fruition. Sometimes, the larger plans can become the premises for smaller plans. For instance, the construction of a new factory creates a need to hire new employees. It is essential that planning premises be consistent and widely understood, so that managers can establish their own plans without contradicting the general plans of the company.

Fourth Step of the Business Planning Process

Once the managers of a business have decided on their objectives and established their planning premises, they must consider the various means of getting the job done. Managers cannot afford to look at an unlimited number of options, so they must determine the critical factor in every situation. The *critical factor* is the one aspect of an operation that will make the most difference. It is sometimes called the limiting factor. Some highly intelligent business managers flail during the planning process because they take too much time weighing alternatives. It is more effective to choose the alternative that offers the best results for the critical factor and accept whatever problems may arise as necessary evils. This problem illustrates the constant struggle in management between doing something right and doing it quickly.

Fifth Step of the Business Planning Process

If all of the steps in the planning process are performed properly, then selecting a course of action should be fairly simple. Unfortunately, it is often the case that real-world choices are not easy. Managers may be concerned about the way the market will change or about the actions of their competitors. Occasionally, it may make sense to delay planning certain future events until external factors can clear up. Some managers will construct a partial plan and leave some choices to be made later once the market develops. Of course, unless this decision to postpone planning is made known to the organization and is sound strategy rather than procrastination, it can result in a rudderless company. One thing is certain: the market will not give time extensions to companies that fail to act.

Sixth Step of the Planning Process

Once a major business plan has been constructed, managers set to work developing all of the supporting plans that will enable the greater plan to be followed. The major plan sets the objectives and premises for all of the smaller or derivative plans. At this point, managers will also need to develop specific budgets for their plans. For a plan to be meaningful to the people with money invested in the business, it must be expressed in its financial form. A proper budget will include the costs of the plan and the number of labor hours that enacting the plan will require. Budgets are important because they set a specific numerical target for a plan and give managers something to measure their actual expenses against. Essentially, budgets are a way of making business planning concrete.

Competing in Foreign Markets

Globalization has made competition in the international market necessary for many corporations. In the past few decades, direct investment from foreign sources has increased tremendously, meaning that national economies are more interrelated than ever.
There are three main ways to compete in foreign markets: investing, exporting, and licensing agreements. Investment is common when businesses want to have influence in a country whose raw materials they desire. Exporting is a common way for companies to initially explore the international market because it offers a relatively low risk if it is done at a minimal level. Licensing agreements are pacts between companies in different countries to market one another's products, or in some other way to engage in mutually beneficial trade.

Environmental Factors' Influence on International Business

There are a large number of social, economic, and political factors that can greatly affect the status of an international business enterprise. Social and cultural concerns, such as the role of each gender within society, along with cultural norms regarding issues such as what types of behavior and what types of appearances are acceptable within the region can profoundly affect how well certain types of products will sell. The current economic conditions of a region are also extremely important to any business. For instance, products that are considered more of a luxury than a necessity will not sell as well in poorer countries.
Political and legal conditions are always an important concern of a business attempting to sell internationally because each country has its own distinct laws, ideological beliefs, and controls on trade. A business that is trading internationally must adhere to the laws, regulations, and political pressures of a particular country if it wishes to trade there.

Environmental Factors to Consider

There are a large number of environmental factors that any company should consider before trading internationally. A major American shaving company might want to consider a number of legal, social, and cultural factors. For example, the company would want to know the cost of shipping overseas, including the cost of tariffs and customs fees, for the country their products are entering. It would also need to understand laws regarding how certain sharp products, such as razor blades, need to be shipped.

There are also a number of social concerns that might arise in advertising a shaving company's products. For example, in the United States, a major shaving company might show an advertisement that contains a large number of clean-shaven men to show off how close a shave their product offers. However, if a company was attempting to sell shaving supplies in a Middle Eastern country, the company would want to show how the razor can be used to groom a beard rather than shave it off because men in those countries are often expected to have long beards.

The Effect of Geographic Factors on International Business

Geographic concerns, such as the ease of access to products, the needs of the consumers in a particular region, and the consumer's access to certain resources, can all affect how well a particular product will sell. If a consumer lives in a region in which it is difficult to get certain products, such as rural areas where there are significant distances between stores or a region that does not have a well-established system of shipping goods, it may be more difficult to sell to that consumer.

The specific needs of the consumer can also be based on the consumer's location. For example, individuals living in a desert region are probably not going to be interested in purchasing a boat. The consumer's access to certain resources can also play a role because individuals that have difficulty finding the resources they require for a product are probably not going to be willing to purchase the product. For instance, someone who does not have easy access to oil and gasoline will probably not buy a car.

Specialization in Relation to International Business

Specialization is the process of separating a particular goal into a series of specific tasks and then focusing the resources available amongst those tasks. For example, an automotive manufacturer might have an assembly line where one individual works the machinery that lowers the engine into the car, one that works the machinery that attaches the tires, one that works the machinery that details the car, and so on. Each of these individuals is a worker that specializes in carrying out a specific task.

Specialization is an important part of international business because it allows companies to produce complex products, such as cars, more quickly and allows companies to change certain small aspects of a product more easily in order to make a product more suitable for a particular region. For example, if a company is producing cars that will be used by consumers in regions with harsh terrain, the company may be able to make the car more appealing simply by changing the tires that the car uses from standard tires to all-terrain tires.

Theory of Comparative Advantage

The *theory of comparative advantage* is a complex concept that is extremely important to any business or nation attempting to conduct international trade. The easiest way to understand this concept is to assume that there are two organizations that are each capable of producing a series of goods, but one of the organizations is capable of producing all of these goods more efficiently than the other organization. Even though one organization is better at producing all of these goods, the comparative advantage theory states that both organizations may still benefit from trading with each other if each organization can specialize in producing a particular good.

For example, if country A can produce a large amount of oil and a large amount of food, but country B produces slightly less oil than country A and significantly less food, both countries may benefit if country A specializes in producing food and country B specializes in producing oil.

Opportunity Costs

An *opportunity cost* refers to the total value of potential gains that are lost from making one decision over any other. In other words, an opportunity cost is anything an individual might have earned from a different option that the individual will not earn from choosing another option. For example, if a business owner is attempting to decide between producing the materials that his business needs or buying the materials from a supplier, the business might want to consider whether or not it could produce more supplies than it needs and sell those additional supplies for a profit. These additional supplies, which might not be available or profitable if the business chose to purchase from a supplier instead, would be an opportunity cost of choosing to use the supplier.

Opportunity costs are extremely important in regard to the theory of comparative advantage because each organization needs to weigh the opportunity costs associated with specializing in a particular area against the gains that they will receive. In international business, the country with the lower opportunity costs for any product will end up with the higher comparative advantage for that product.

Types of Economic Systems in the International Marketplace

The four major types of economic systems currently found in the world are traditional economies, market economies, command economies, and mixed economies.

Traditional economies are economic systems that are based primarily on cultural beliefs and traditions and are frequently found in less-industrialized nations. Nations with traditional economies are usually concerned primarily with producing basic necessities. They typically focus heavily on food production activities.

Market economies are economic systems in which private individuals produce and distribute the goods and services that can be found in the marketplace.

Command economies, also known as *planned economies*, are economies in which only the government has the authority to produce and distribute the goods and services that can be found in the marketplace.

Mixed economies are economies with a combination of market and command economies. Some businesses are privately owned, whereas other businesses are owned and operated solely by the government.

Locations of the Four Types of Economic Systems

Traditional economies are usually used in less-developed nations, such as the poorer nations of Asia, Africa, and South America. Examples include Haiti, Rwanda, and certain African and South American tribes.

Market economies are usually found in capitalist and free enterprise societies such as Japan, the United Kingdom, and the United States.

Command economies are usually found in communist and socialist societies such as North Korea, the former Soviet Union, and Cuba.

Mixed economies are somewhat more difficult to identify because even though certain countries are often classified as using market economies such as the United States or command economies such as China, most nations actually use a combination of the two. For example, even though the United States primarily uses a market economic system, it could be classified as using a mixed economic system because certain utilities and industries are owned or subsidized by the government.

Traditional and Market Economic Systems' Effects on International Trade

Each of the four types of economic systems—traditional, market, command, and mixed—function in a different way, and the type of economic system that a nation uses can greatly influence the ease of trading in a particular country.

Traditional economies are usually poorer, do not readily accept change, and usually do not encourage free trade, so it is more difficult for international businesses to conduct trade in these nations. Even if a business is able to trade in a nation with a traditional economy, it is unlikely that the business will be able to find enough consumers with the resources available to purchase its products and services.

Market economies, on the other hand, usually have more resources, are reasonably more flexible to change, and heavily encourage free trade, so it is significantly easier for international businesses to trade in market economies. As a result, the primary problem that arises from trading in a market economy is that each business has significantly more competition.

Command and Mixed Economic Systems' Effects on International Trade

Command and mixed economies, just as traditional and market economies, can have profound effects on the ease with which a business conducts trade within the country. Command economies may possess the resources necessary to conduct trade, but by their very nature, forbid free trade. Also, they are often resistant to change, so it may be difficult or even impossible for outside businesses to conduct trade with consumers within a command economy.

Mixed economies allow for a reasonable amount of flexibility to change because they consist of a combination of both a command and market economic system. Each nation with a mixed economy offers a differing level of free trade, depending on the laws and regulations set by the government. Most of the world's larger nations use a mixed economic system and, therefore, businesses dealing internationally need to have at least a basic understanding of the laws and regulations of each country to continue trading.

Country's Imports and Exports Effects on International Trade

An understanding of the basic goods that a country has available to export and the basic goods that the country needs to regularly import can be extremely useful for any international business. By observing the exporting and importing habits of a particular nation, a business can determine which products the country has in ample supply and which products are in demand. This allows a business trading internationally to purchase goods from countries and businesses that have an overabundance of a particular good. The overabundance allows the business to purchase these products more cheaply than it could in regions where the supply does not meet the demand. These international businesses can then sell those products to regions and consumers that have a shortage of that particular product to make a profit.

It is also important that any business trading internationally understands the laws of the country in which they are operating and the country into which they are shipping goods because each country has different regulations regarding imports and exports.

Foreign Exchange Markets' Role in International Trade

Foreign exchange markets play a pivotal role within international trade because there are a large number of businesses from a variety of different countries trading within the international marketplace at all times. Foreign exchange markets allow a business to exchange one nation's currency for the currency of another nation, which is extremely important because different nations use different currencies, and the value of those currencies is largely dependent upon the economic and political state of the country they are used in. As a result, the value associated with each type of currency in the marketplace can change extremely quickly, and there may be times that trading with a certain country may not be as profitable as trading with another country, even though the price of the product has remained the same. This is because the consumer's currency, even though the consumer is paying the price that the business set for that particular product, is actually worth less than the same amount of currency from a different country.

Business Techniques and Practices

Many of the major techniques and practices commonly used by domestic businesses can also be applied to businesses trading internationally. In fact, techniques such as quality control and total quality management can be extremely important, as laws regarding product quality and safety vary from country to country. Any business that wishes to trade internationally not only needs to be aware of the laws and regulations surrounding the type of product the business is attempting to sell, but also able to meet those regulations effectively and efficiently.
Practices such as quality control, which ensures that the product meets the legal guidelines set by the nation's government, and total quality management, which makes sure that all of the businesses procedures are carried out as effectively as possible, can be easily applied to products traded both domestically and internationally. Most common business and marketing techniques, practices, and strategies can be applied to international trade simply by having an understanding of the needs and laws of the consumer's nation.

Resources Available in the State of Georgia

The American state of Georgia possesses a large number of financial, human, natural, and transportation resources that are all important to the state's international trade. The state of Georgia usually has a thriving economy, as indicated by the state's relatively high gross state product, and has significant financial resources as a result. Georgia's large and rapidly growing population also allows the state to have a large workforce available. There are also a large number of natural resources in Georgia, including vast amounts of land suitable for agricultural industries, such as the production of peaches, peanuts, poultry, eggs, and other dairy products, as well as a large number of clay, granite, sand, and stone deposits. In addition, the state has a significant amount of woodland areas suitable for logging. Finally, Georgia also has a number of transportation resources, and the state's capital of Atlanta acts as a transportation hub because it is at the center of several major highways and is equipped with a major international airport and a series of railroad terminals.

Georgia's International Trading Partners

The state of Georgia has a number of international trading partners that trade on a frequent basis with the businesses of the state. These trading partners include a variety of different businesses in a number of different countries. Most of these trading partners are located in Australia, China, Germany, Ireland, Italy, Japan, Malaysia, the Netherlands, South Korea, and the United Kingdom. These international trading partners make it possible for Georgia to acquire the resources, supplies, and equipment that the businesses in the state require to continue functioning. Some of the common goods and resources imported into Georgia include electrical machinery, industrial machinery, computers, cars and other vehicles, mineral fuel, oil, and pharmaceutical products.

Risks Associated with International Trade

There are a large number of economic and political risks associated with any business trading internationally. Some of the most significant economic risks associated with international trade include a buyer not having the resources to pay for a particular product and that the buyer may agree to certain terms and then renege on the agreement, leaving the business with little or no recourse.
It is also important for a nation or business considering trade with another country to consider the risk of becoming dependent upon importing a particular good or resource from another nation, rather than producing it domestically. Some of the most significant political and legal risks associated with international trade include the risk of war breaking out in a particular region and the risk that laws in the region might change, possibly hindering the business' ability to do business. The potential losses that a business might suffer if a country bans a particular good after it has already been shipped can also be a major concern.

Planning an International Business Venture

There are several procedures that an individual or organization can use to plan an international business venture. One of the most useful of such procedures is that of a risk assessment. To perform a risk assessment, a business must first determine which countries they want to conduct business in and then conduct research on the laws, regulations, economic status, and societal norms of those nations. The business can then either hire an outside company to perform a risk assessment or perform an assessment internally by constructing a list of all the major risks associated with the venture. The business can then either decide that the risks of the venture outweigh the potential gains of the venture and call the venture off, or implement risk management strategies to lower the risk of certain problems arising from the venture in the future.

Major International Economic Institutions and the Global Economy

Major international economic institutions, such as the World Trade Organization, the International Monetary Fund, and the World Bank, are all extremely important to the global economy because they help set the foundations for international trade. These organizations primarily act as overseers that supervise the basic elements necessary for nations and individual businesses to trade internationally. They also attempt to make sure that individuals, businesses, and entire nations have the information they need to continue making intelligent trading decisions.

The World Trade Organization sets the rules and regulations that its member nations are expected to follow when carrying out trade negotiations. It also makes sure that, once an agreement is reached, both nations uphold their side of the agreement.

The International Monetary Fund supervises the international financial system by monitoring both the changes in exchange rates and the payments being made from one country to another.

The World Bank primarily acts as an advisor to the poorer nations of the world, attempting to improve their economies and eliminate poverty.

Growth and Importance of International Trade

While there are a variety of reasons that international trade has grown exceptionally well over time, the most important reasons include improvements to transportation and communication, improvements to procedures and goods-producing equipment, and a steady rise in consumer income.

The introduction of fleets of commercial cargo planes, ships, and other modes of transportation have improved transportation, while the introduction of the Internet was a communication breakthrough. Both of these improvements have made it far easier for businesses and nations to conduct trade with international partners.

Also, improvements to the procedures and equipment used to produce various goods have allowed industrialized nations to produce products both faster and cheaper than in the past. Finally, many consumers across the world are earning more money, allowing them to purchase more goods. As a result, international trade has become an important part of the global economy because it allows individuals, businesses, and nations to acquire goods that are cheaper, unavailable in a particular region, or help meet the demand of the consumers.

Information Technology

Most Common Types of Business Software

Businesses use a variety of different software packages to help them accomplish tasks quickly and accurately. Most businesses use some variation of the Office XP package, which includes programs for word processing, spreadsheets, databases, and PowerPoint presentations. Businesses may also use more sophisticated spreadsheet programs, like Excel, or more advanced graphics programs. The accounting department may have special software to help them keep track of financial records, and there are many payroll programs to help monitor employee payment. Many businesses have their own unique computer programs to manage inventory and workflow.

Specialized Types of Business and Software

Some businesses need to access certain information because of their unique function. Medical and legal businesses, for example, often use sophisticated transcription software to give them access to records and references. Many businesses that used to have extensive filing systems, in which hard copies were stored, now keep all of their records electronically. They are then, of course, susceptible to the dangers of a computer malfunction; for this reason, most small businesses have some sort of backup disk where duplicate copies of records are kept. Large businesses often have a contract with their computer provider to create a duplicate computer system in case of operating system malfunction.

Basics of Word Processing

Word processing is the use of computers to compose, store, edit, and publish text. Before the advent of word processing, creating business documents was an incredibly tedious job. Word processors are most typically used to produce memos and letters, thus facilitating the flow of information around an office. However, they are also useful for constructing databases, spreadsheets, and charts. Studies have indicated that the introduction of word processors has encouraged people to write more, if perhaps not better. There appears to be a tendency to adopt a more conversational tone in word processing than is always appropriate for business communications. There are a few health concerns related to the frequent use of word processors, including eyestrain and carpal-tunnel syndrome.

Creating a New Document in Word

There are four different ways to begin a new document in Word. One way is simply to start up the Word program; the program will open with a blank document. Another way is to click on the button for New Blank Document in the Standard toolbar. Yet another way to create a blank document is to click File, and then New, while you are in Word. Finally, you can press Control + N. If you would like to use a document template (a blank document with paragraphs and headings already formatted), simply create a new document and then click on the General Templates icon, bringing up the Templates dialog box. You will then be provided with a list of templates from which you can choose.

Entering Text into a Document in Word

The two most common ways to enter text into a document are by typing it in or by importing it from another document. Typing is fairly easy in Word, because the AutoCorrect feature alerts the user to potential misspellings and misuses of grammar. Word will correct the spelling of obviously misspelled words, but it will also ask you about words that it believes may be misspelled. It can learn new words, too. Importing text from another document is a simple process: select Copy from the menu or toolbar and move the text from the display window of the original program to the display window of the Word document. It may be necessary when using some programs to save the original text in a new format that is acceptable to Word.

Ways to View a Word Document

Word gives you a few different ways to look at your document, depending on what you are trying to accomplish. There are four ways to look at a basic document, all of which are accessible from the View menu. The Normal mode is appropriate for periods of typing: it allows you to work on an essentially clean screen without any headers or footers. When you view your document in Web layout, you are seeing what it will look like as a Web page. Print layout has a similar function: it shows you what your document will look like when it is printed. Outline format is fairly self-explanatory; it is the appropriate view for creating an outline to organize data and text.

Scroll Bars, Screen Magnification, and Paragraph Marks

Sometimes, you may want to open up a little space in a Word document by removing the horizontal and vertical scroll bars. To do this, click Tools, then Options, to display the Options dialog box. Under the View tab, uncheck the boxes for the two scroll bars and click OK. If you would like to change the magnification of the screen, click View, and then Zoom, to display the Zoom dialog box. A number of percentages will be displayed, along with a setting for Page Width, which will make the line of text however long the Word window is at present. Sometimes, you may want a visual representation of the spacing or the paragraph marks in your document. You can display or hide these by clicking on the paragraph symbol (a backwards P with two vertical lines) on the toolbar.

Standard Toolbar in Word

In order to prevent the user from having constantly to access the menu to perform tasks, Word has developed the Standard toolbar to make a number of common functions accessible by a simple mouse click. The Standard toolbar contains Word's most frequently used commands, beginning with New Blank Document (symbolized by a white sheet of paper), Open (an open file folder), Save (a floppy diskette), E-mail (an envelope and letter), Search (magnifying glass on document with Windows symbol), Print (printer), Preview (magnifying glass on blank document), Spelling and Grammar check (check mark and ABC), Cut (scissors), Copy (two documents), Paste (jar of paste), Format Painter (paintbrush), Undo (arrow looping left), and Redo (arrow looping right).

Buttons on the Standard Toolbar

Word has a large and various toolbar, allowing the user to accomplish a number of different tasks without dealing with a menu. Working from left to right, the buttons that come after the Redo command are Insert Hyperlink (depicted as Earth and infinity symbol), Tables and Borders (four-part square with pencil), Insert Table (graph document with blue header), Insert Microsoft Excel Worksheet (graph document with green *X*), Columns (two sets of horizontal lines), Drawing (*A* with cube and cylinder), Document Map (magnifying glass on document with blue header), Show/Hide paragraph marks (paragraph symbol), Zoom (display screen for current magnification setting), Help (question mark), and More Buttons (small down arrow).

Buttons on the Formatting Toolbar

In order to make formatting tasks easier, Word has a comprehensive toolbar that allows the user to perform tasks with the click of a mouse. The buttons on this toolbar are, from left to right: Style (a display window names the current text style), Font (similar display window), Font Size (display window), Bold (bold *B*), Italics (italicized *I*), Underline (underlined *U*), Align Left, Align Right, and Justify (all symbolized by a representation of their format), Line Spacing (up and down arrows and horizontal lines), Numbering (*1*, *2*, and *3* next to text), Bullets (blue squares next to text), Decrease Indent (arrow moving text left), Increase Indent (arrow moving text right), Outside Border (square), Highlight (highlighter), Font Color (*A* with red underline), and More Buttons (small down arrow).

Ruler Tabs in Word

In Word, the ruler is the numbered bar along the side of the document that defines the margins and the tabs of the document. You can use the ruler to change the margins or the indenture. To hide or display the ruler, click View, then Ruler. There are five different tabs displayed on the ruler. The left tab, which resembles an *L*, moves the text to the right edge of the page as you type. The center tab, which looks like an upside-down *T*, centers the text around the tab. The right tab, which looks like a backward *L*, moves text towards the left edge of the page. The decimal tab, which looks like an inverted *T* with a dot next to it), aligns all of the numbers in a column by the decimal point. The bar tab, which looks like a straight vertical line, draws a vertical line on the document.

Using Indents in Word

The Tab Selection button in Word has a couple of different options that allow the user to manipulate paragraph indentions. The First Line Indent icon, which looks like an inverted house, allows you to set the left margin of the first line in every paragraph. The Hanging Indent icon is a big *U* on the Tab Selection button, and a house above the Left Indent button on the ruler. It allows the user to set the left margin for every line by the first in a paragraph. There are two other indentation options on the ruler, represented by the Left and Right Indent icons. These allow you to define the left and right margins of every line in a particular paragraph. It should be noted that the ruler can only display one indent per paragraph.

Ways to Move Through a Word Document

There are a few different ways to navigate through a Word document. The quickest way is usually just to use the mouse. The vertical scroll bar on the right side of the screen allows you to quickly scroll up or down (the single arrows) or to move up or down a page at a time (the double arrows). The keyboard can also be used to navigate a Word document: the arrows move the cursor, obviously, but by pressing Ctrl + the up or down arrow you can jump up or down a paragraph at a time. When you know exactly where you want to go in a document, it may be most efficient to use the Go To command. This command can take you to a specific line number, page number, or bookmark, simply by pressing Ctrl + G.

Text Selection with a Mouse

In order to work with text in a Word document, you first have to know how to select that text with the mouse or keyboard. The easiest way to select text is by dragging the mouse: just drag the mouse from one end of the desired text to the other, with the left button of the mouse held down. There are some more sophisticated ways to select text with a mouse in Word: double-clicking at the beginning of a word selects that word and the space after it; holding down the Ctrl key and clicking inside a sentence will select that entire sentence; triple-clicking inside a paragraph will select that entire paragraph; clicking to the far left of a line of the first word in a line will select that whole line; and double-clicking to the far left of a paragraph will select the entire paragraph.

Text Selection with a Keyboard

Sometimes, it is more convenient or precise to select text with the keyboard rather than the mouse. There are a few essential key commands for selecting text. Pressing Shift + the right or left arrow selects the character to the right or left of the cursor. Shift + Home selects all of the current line to the left of the cursor, while Shift + End selects all of the text to the right of the cursor. Shift + Page Up or Page Down selects a screenful of text either above or below the cursor. Ctrl + Shift + the right or left arrow selects the word to the right or left of the cursor, while Ctrl + Shift + Home or End selects all of the text from the cursor to either the beginning or end of the document. Ctrl + A selects the entire document.

Deleting Text in a Word Document

Two keys can be used to delete text in a Word document. The Backspace key will delete characters to the left of the cursor, while the Delete key will eliminate characters to the right of the cursor. Words are often deleted by an accidental press of the Insert key. This key will shift the computer from Insert mode, in which new typing in the middle of a document will push the old typing to the right, to Overtype mode, in which new type goes over whatever had been there before. If you would like to undo an accidental or ill-advised deletion, simply click Edit, then Undo, or just click the Undo icon (an arrow looping left) in the Standard toolbar. This command will reverse your last command.

Copying and Moving Text in a Word Document

Sometimes, you may want to duplicate part of a document, or move chunks of text from one area of a document to another. To do this, first select the text that you would like to manipulate. Then you may either cut or copy the selected text: cutting will remove the text from this location, whereas copying will keep the text where it is while allowing you to reproduce it elsewhere in the document. Both these tasks can be performed by right-clicking on the selected text and choosing from the pop-up menu. Now, move the cursor to the spot where you would like to place the text and Paste it, either by right-clicking and choosing Paste, or by clicking the Paste icon in the Standard toolbar.

Search/Replace and Spell Check in Word Processing

There are a few basic word processing commands that every business student needs to know. The Search/Replace command enables the user to find a particular word or phrase in a document, and then replace it with another word. The Search function is particularly useful for finding common misspellings or overused words. Spell check is another command that students will find very useful. It orders the word processing program to look through the document for misspelled words. There is always a danger, of course, that students will rely too heavily on the spell check command. The computer may identify unfamiliar words as misspelled, and may recommend new spellings that deviate from the word originally intended by the student.

Spell Check and Grammar Check in Word

The Word program will alert you to possible errors in spelling or grammar. A green wavy line indicates a possible grammatical error, while a wavy red line indicates a possible spelling mistake. To address these problems, right-click the mouse while the pointer is over the word or sentence in question. A pop-up box will appear, in which Word will describe the problem it sees and suggest a solution. For spelling mistakes, you may agree with Word's suggested spellings, or you may indicate to Word that the word is spelled correctly, but is simply unknown to the computer. On questions of grammar, you may accept the solution offered by Word, you may make your own changes in a display box and enter them into the document, or you may tell Word to ignore the error.

How to Find and Replace Text

One of the useful features of the Word program is that it allows you to find a particular word and phrase every time it appears in a document. To find a word, click Edit, then Find, or simply press Ctrl + F. At this point, a Find and Replace dialog box will appear. Enter the word or phrase you are looking for in the Find What box, or click on the down arrow to see a list of your recent searches. After you press Find Next, the program will find the first instance in the text. Then, if you would like to replace the text, enter the new text into the Replace With box. By clicking Find Next, you will substitute the text. If you are absolutely certain it is appropriate, you may select Replace All to have every instance of the original text replaced.

Adjusting the Font

One of the ways you can personalize your documents is by adjusting the font (the appearance of each letter). Word is equipped with a wide array of fonts, which can be accessed by clicking the Font list box on the Formatting toolbar. It should be noted that choosing a font will have an effect on the size of the type; some fonts must be shown in a large format, whereas others are more appropriate for small print. For the most part, business documents will be in either Times New Roman or MS Sans Serif. To change the font of a particular section of text, simply highlight the text, click the Font list box on the Formatting toolbar, and select your font. You may also want to adjust the font size by clicking on the Font Size list box on the same toolbar.

Aligning Text

Word allows you to align the text of your document. Although most documents should be aligned to the left, it is sometimes appropriate to set up a group of words in another way. Word gives you four options for aligning text: left-align, center-align, right-align, and justify. When text is left-aligned, the left margin will be a straight line, while the right line will be uneven. In a right-aligned document, the format is exactly the opposite. In a centered text, each line is centered in the middle of the page, so that both the right and left margins are uneven. When text is justified, both the left and right margins are straight; words may need to be somewhat unnaturally spaced to achieve this. All of these alignments can be accessed from the Formatting toolbar.

Text Indention and Format Painter

It may occasionally be a good idea to indent a certain chunk of text in a Word document, perhaps to set it off from the rest of the text. In academic papers, long quotations are often indented to distinguish them from the work of the author. In order to do this, first select the text you would like to indent; Word will indent an entire paragraph even if you only highlight a section. Then, click the Indent or Decrease Indent buttons to move the text to either the right or the left. If you are pleased with the formatting on a particular piece of text, and would like to have the same formatting on another piece of text, you may use the Format Painter on the Formatting toolbar. To do this, highlight the first batch of text and click the paintbrush icon on the toolbar; then, select the text you would like to format.

Formatting Template

Rather than force you to make every formatting decision on a document, Word is equipped with a few shortcuts that allow you to select some commonly used formats. There are three main decisions that a user must make when settling on a formatting template: themes, style templates, and general style. By adjusting the theme, the user is adjusting the color and appearance of the numbers, bullets, horizontal lines, or background of a document. The style templates are simple formats for common documents, like fax cover pages, resumes, and business letters. By adjusting the style, the user is altering the format for particular paragraphs, including the margins, font size, and any underlining.

Theme Dialog Box

Word allows the user to adjust the decorative appearance of a document, otherwise known as the theme. To choose a theme, click on Format, then Theme, calling up the Theme dialog box. Once there, you can select a theme from the Choose a Theme list (Word will provide you with a sample of that theme when you click on it). By checking various boxes, you may add or remove colors in the document, add or remove graphics to make the document livelier, and add or remove a background picture. Once you have settled on a theme, clicking OK will apply it to the document. Altering the theme of a Word document does not make any substantial change to the content; it is only appropriate when you want a more attractive presentation.

Style Template

If you are creating a common sort of document in Word, you may want to use a style template. There are style templates available for faxes, memos, proposals, cover letters, resumes, and other frequently used documents. To select a style template, simply click on Format, and then Theme. Once the Theme dialog box appears, click on the Style Gallery button, which will display the Style Gallery dialog box. Here, you can scroll through and select one of the common style templates. By clicking Document, you can see what your present document will look like with the selected format; clicking Example will show you how a generic document looks in the selected format; clicking Style Samples will create an array of the various styles that make up that template.

Paragraph Formatting with Different Styles

When you alter the Style of a Word document, you are altering the general appearance of the text, including the font and the size of the type. To select a style, simply utilize the Style box on the Formatting toolbar. First, move the cursor to whatever paragraph you would like to be affected by the formatting. If you haven't typed anything, Word will format whatever you type next. Some of the commonly-used formats are for a signature, for a subject heading, for a numbered list, or for a return address. Simply click on the style you would like to use and Word will format it immediately. This is a useful method of formatting if you are composing a simple business document but do not want to use a comprehensive style template that affects every aspect.

List Set-up

At some point, you may want to use Word to create a list for work or for your personal life. You can make two different sorts of lists: numbered or bulleted. To set up a list, first select the text you would like to have made into a list. If you do not select any text, Word will turn whatever text you type next into a list. Click Format, then Bullets and Numbering, which will bring up the Bullets and Numbering dialog box. This box will provide a set of numbered or bulleted list types, from which you can choose. Once you have selected the type of list you prefer, clicking OK will immediately convert the text into that list format. If you don't really care what style of list Word uses, just click the Numbering or Bullets icon in the Formatting toolbar and start typing. This will tell Word to start a list in the default format.

Adding Headers and Footers

Users of Word can make their documents look more sophisticated by adding headers and footers containing the publication title, chapter title, page number, or author's name. Adding headers and footers allows you to include this helpful information without having to type it on every page. To view the headers and footers, either click View, then Header and Footer, or View, then Print Layout. To add a header or footer, select View, then Header and Footer, to display the Header and Footer text box. You can then type whatever text you would like, or click a button to have Word display the date, page number, or number of pages. You can also toggle between Header and Footer on this screen.

Page Numbering

If you simply tell Word to number the pages in a document, it will print an Arabic numeral (that is, 1, 2, 3...) on each page. You may want to modify the numbering, however, to begin at a certain page or to be expressed in Roman numerals or letters. To do this, you have to use the Page Number Format button on the Header and Footer toolbar. First, select View, then Header and Footer, calling up the Header and Footer toolbar. Next, highlight the page numbers that appear in either the Header or Footer text box. Click on the Format Page Number button to bring up the Page Number Format dialog box. The options in this box will allow you to select a page numbering style, or to designate where you would like the page numbering to begin.

Inserting Graphics into a Word Document

There are several different ways to insert graphics into a Word document. By using the Clip Art feature, you can insert any picture from the Clip Art gallery. You can also insert graphics by calling up those that have been stored in files from other programs. Using the AutoShapes command will draw one of many generic shapes in the document. Using WordArt gives you the chance to create text in different colors and shapes. You can also use the New Drawing command to create original drawings from geometric shapes, lines, and WordArt. Word gives you the option to add digital images that have been created by a scanner or a digital camera. The Chart command allows you to add a chart or graph to represent data.

Clip-art

Clip-art is ready-made imagery that can be easily inserted into a Word document. Office XP will organize all of the clip-art in various programs into a comprehensive Media Gallery. Before you can start adding clip-art to your documents, you have to tell the Media Gallery which folders you would like to search for art. After you click Insert, then Picture, and then Clip Art, the Add Clips to Gallery button will appear. By clicking on the Options button, an Auto Import Settings button will emerge, which will display all of the folders in which Media Gallery can search for pictures. Once you have selected all of the appropriate folders, you can click Catalog and the Media gallery will organize your clip-art.

Adding Clip-art to a Document

Adding clip-art to a text document is an easy way to enhance the appearance. To do so, first select Insert, then Picture, then Clip Art. This will bring up the Insert Clip Art window. From there, you can type into the Search text box a few words that describe the clip art that you would like. Once you have selected the image you would like to display, move the cursor to the point in the Word document where you would like to insert the graphic. Then, click the down arrow next to the image, calling up a short menu. From this menu, click Insert. Once you have confirmed that your chosen graphic has been inserted into the document, you may close the Insert Clip Art window.

Inserting Already-Existing Graphic Files and Auto Shapes

Word makes it quite easy to insert your own graphics into a Word document. All you have to do is place the cursor where you would like to insert the image, and select Insert, then

Picture, and then From File. After the Insert Picture dialog box appears, find the file you would like to insert and click Insert. Word also has a set of basic shapes (square, circles, ovals) that you can insert into a document. To place these Auto Shapes into your document, move the cursor to the appropriate location and click Insert, then Picture, then Auto Shapes. This will bring up an Auto Shapes toolbar, from which you can select an image. Then, move the mouse back to the right spot, hold down the left button, and drag the mouse over to indicate how large you would like the graphic to be.

Manipulating a Picture around Text

Sometimes, a graphic that is inserted into a text document may have the unpleasant effect of covering up the text underneath. To remedy this situation, click on the picture and hit the right mouse button, calling up a pop-up menu. Select Format, and when the Format dialog box appears, go to the Layout tab. Select a style of text wrapping from the available options, and click OK. If you need to move a picture within a document, just click on the picture, so that the handles become evident around it. Then, hold down the left mouse button as you drag the mouse pointer to the place where you would like the graphic to appear. Releasing the left mouse button will place the graphic in the desired location.

How Formatting is Checked

Formatting a document in Word can be a tricky process, so it is never a bad idea to take a look at your work before you print your document. If you notice an area of text that is incorrect, you can check its formatting by using the Reveal Formatting pane. To access this pane, highlight the text you are interested in adjusting and click Format, then Reveal Formatting. This will bring up the Reveal Formatting pane. Here, you can select Show All Formatting Marks, which will allow you to see every single space and paragraph mark in your document. If necessary, you can make adjustments to Alignment, Font, or other formatting aspects by clicking on the appropriate link. Clicking on the Close box will cause the Reveal Formatting pane to disappear.

Mail Merge

The Mail Merge feature in Word allows you to send a standard letter to a list of different people or businesses. To do so, click Tools, then Mail Merge, bringing up the Mail Merge Helper dialog box. If your document is already set up, you can go ahead and click on Data Source (otherwise, use the Main document feature to set up). The Create Data Source dialog box will open, allowing you to enter the information you would like to include for each recipient. When you are satisfied with the various fields, click on Save As, then List, and Word will proceed to the screen on which you will enter the data for each of your recipients. Once you have finished entering all of the data, just go to the Insert Merge Field menu and place the various fields where you would like them. When you print the document, the computer should print a different copy for each recipient.

Saving a Document

To save a document in Word, you can press Ctrl + S; click the Save button on the Standard toolbar; or click File, then Save. If you are saving a document for the first time, you will be asked to enter a name for the file. Sometimes, you may want to save a document under a new name or as a different type of file. To do this, simply open the document and then click

- 56 -

File, then Save As. Type a new name for your file in the File Name box, or select a new file type from the list in the Save As Type box. This may be appropriate of you are going to have to use the file in another program, like WordPerfect. File names cannot contain slashes, backslashes, question marks, quotation marks, colons, or semicolons.

Using the Backup Feature

For users who worry that their system may be unstable, Word has included an easy way to create an automatic backup copy of a document. This backup feature will create a duplicate copy of a document every time it is saved. The backup copy will be called "Backup of [file name]," and will be stored in the same folder as the original document. To turn on the backup feature, select the Tool menu, and then click on Options. This will call up the Options dialog box. Here, click on the Save tab and, once there, make sure that there is a check mark in the Always Create Backup Copy box. Creating a backup file may allow you to retrieve data in the event of a computer crash.

Steps for Printing a Word Document

When you think that you are ready to print a completed Word document, it is always a good idea to use the Print Preview first. To do this, select File, then Print Preview. A display window will be created, in which you can survey the document to ensure that it is ready to be printed. Before printing, you may want to define the page margins and paper size; this can be done by accessing the Page Setup dialog box under the File menu. Once you are ready to print, click on File, then Print (or just press Ctrl + P), to bring up the Print dialog box. Make sure that the right printer is selected, and that the computer is set to print the right pages. You can also adjust the number of copies that will be printed. Once you are satisfied with the print settings, clicking on OK will begin printing.

Common Proofreading Symbols Used to Edit Copy

Proofreaders in the United States have developed a set of simple symbols and abbreviations to quickly annotate documents and indicate necessary changes. Some of the most common of these are as follows: a caret (^; means insert something here); a number sign (#; insert a space); slash (/; delete), eq + number sign (space evenly); *stet* (let stand); *tr* (transpose); [(set farther to the left);] (set farther to the right); = (align horizontally); // (align vertically); paragraph symbol (¶; start a new paragraph); *cap* (put into capital letters); *sp* (spelling error); and *OK?* (note to author, asking "Is this what you meant?").

Starting a Database in Works

There are a couple of different ways to start a database in Works. The first way is to double-click the Works shortcut on the desktop screen, and then click the Database icon at the top of the screen. The other way is to click Start, and then select Programs, Microsoft Works, and Microsoft Works Database. Once the program starts, you will be asked to select a blank database, a template, or an existing database. If you want to define each field in your new database, you should select a blank database. If you would like to pick from a list of pre-existing databases, simply select a template. If you would like to make adjustments or additions to a database that you have already constructed, select an existing database.

Controls on the Works Database Window

The main window in the Works database program has a number of adjustable elements. The menu is simply the menu system found in all other Works programs. The toolbar has a number of the menu options available for instant access. The editing window shows all of the data values contained in a record, and allows the user to alter them. The list of records will appear only in List view. In this format, each row represents a single record. The Zoom control allows the user to magnify or shrink the scale of the database. The status bar gives help in the event of an abnormal entry, and also tells you whether you have the Caps Lock and Num Lock buttons depressed.

Creating the First Field of a New Database

Works provides a wizard dialog box system to help you begin a new database. The first step is to type the name of the first field in the Field Name box. You will then enter the format for that field; that is, whether the field will contain numbers, words, or something else. This enables Works to alert you if you make an abnormal entry later in the database. You may be asked whether data fields should include a default value; that is, if there is likely to be a certain value that is used most of the time in that field. Once all this is done, you can click the Add button. Works will then enter a column on the database for the field you have just created, and will clear the dialog box so that you can begin working on a new field.

Editing a Database in Works

One of the best things about a database is to the ease of modifying information that is found to be incorrect. You may use either List or Form view to make changes. First, navigate to the record that needs to be changed. In List view, this is done by scrolling; in Form view, you may either search for the record or use the Record box. Then, click on the field that needs to be changed and press F2. At this point, the program will switch to Edit mode. Then, type the new data value, and press enter to save the changes to the data value and update the field. It should be noted that the user can correct fields as well as specific values in Works; by selecting Insert Field, a new field can be entered between already existing fields.

Ways to Find and Organize Records in Works

There are a couple of different ways to find and organize records in a Works database. To sort records, click Record, then Sort Records. At this point, Works will show a dialog box, from which the user can select what criteria he or she would like the records to be sorted by (for example, last name, descending order, ascending order). The beauty of the computer database is that it can instantly sort data, so the user can try out a number of different arrangements depending on his or her interest. If he or she just wants to find a particular record, this can be done by clicking Edit, then Find, to display the Find dialog box. Then, the user simply types the text that he or she is looking for, and Works will locate it.

Works Database Report

Databases not only store and display data, they are also capable of producing database reports. Creating a report in Works is a simple process. First, click Tools, then Report Creator. This will call up the first screen of the Report Creator. Enter a name for the new report and select OK to continue, bringing up the Report Creator dialog box. Then, choose whether the report should be presented in Portrait or Landscape format. Next, select the fields that you would like to be included in the report. Then, use the Sorting tab to determine how you would like the data to be arranged. Then, enter any summaries of data that you would like the program to make, as for instance if you would like certain values to be added together. At this point, you can generate the report by clicking Report view.

How to Print Databases in Works

Sometimes it is handy to have a hard copy of a particular database you have created in Works. You can print out lists of records, you can print out the records as forms, or you can print out any reports that you have generated. It is always a good idea to click File, then Print, rather than just clicking the Print icon in the toolbar, so that you can double-check that the print settings are appropriate. Once you have selected File, then Print, a Print dialog box will be displayed. In this dialog, you can specify the kind of document you would like, as well as any specifications that should be made and the number of copies that you would like to have printed. This dialog box can also be accessed by pressing Control + P.

Spreadsheets

Spreadsheets are computer files in which numbers can be manipulated and put into graphical form. Many business teachers find them especially useful when teaching basic accounting principles. One of the advantages of computer spreadsheet programs is that numbers can be changed easily, allowing students to construct various hypothetical situations. For example, a teacher might ask students to develop basic profit and loss accounts for a business, and then see how varying amounts of sales and production costs affect the final profit or loss. Students can implement simple formulae on spreadsheets, such that data can be plugged in to generate an immediate answer. Spreadsheets, then, are a great way to help students master the fundamentals of some rather dry accounting subjects.

Starting a Spreadsheet in Works

Spreadsheets are invaluable for any number of tasks, from arranging a budget to making financial forecasts. The spreadsheet program in Works is generally considered to be simpler than Excel, and therefore a better learning tool for introductory business students. In order to start a spreadsheet in Works, you may double-click the Works shortcut on the desktop to run the Task Launcher. Then, click the Spreadsheet icon at the top of the screen. Another way to access the program is by double-clicking a Works Spreadsheet document in Explorer, or on your desktop. A third way is to click Start, then Programs, then Works, then Works Spreadsheet. Instead of pressing Start, one can always press one of the Windows keys on the keyboard.

Features of the Spreadsheet Window

The spreadsheet window in Works has a few features that even the casual user should understand. The menu, at the top of the screen, includes all the commands typical of a Works program. The toolbar (there is only one for spreadsheet applications) allows the user to access certain commands without going to the menu. The editing window, at the bottom of the screen, has all of the spreadsheet cells for numbers, text, graphics, or formulas. The row and column header buttons select entire rows at a time, and allow you to adjust the dimensions. The Zoom control allows the user to magnify or shrink the screen. The status bar suggests possible commands, and indicates whether the Caps Lock and Num Lock buttons are selected.

Navigating and Entering Data in a Works Spreadsheet

There are a number of shortcut keys that can be used in Works to avoid having constantly to shift between keyboard and mouse. The essential keyboard commands for spreadsheet use are the arrows (move the cursor from cell to cell), Home (moves the cursor to the beginning of the row), Ctrl + Home (moves the cursor to the beginning of the worksheet), Ctrl + End (moves the cursor to the last cell in the worksheet that contains a value), Page Up and Page Down (move the cursor from screen to screen), Enter (moves the cursor one cell down), Tab (moves the cursor one cell to the right), Shift + Enter (moves the cursor one cell up), Shift + Tab (moves the cursor one cell to the left), and Ctrl + Arrow key (moves the cursor to the last cell in any range that contains data).

Selecting and Editing Cells

Usually, it is most efficient to select cells in the Works spreadsheet with the mouse. To select a single cell, simply click on that cell. In order to select a range of cells, click on a cell at one end of the range and drag the mouse in the appropriate direction. To select a column of cells, click on the alphabetic heading button at the top of the column. To select a row of cells, just click the numeric heading button on the left side of the row. After the appropriate cell or range has been selected, the contents can be edited by simply deleting them, adding text or numbers to them, or copying data from another cell into the selected one.

Number Format in Works Spreadsheets

When a user works with the number format in a spreadsheet, he or she is adjusting how the cell will display numbers; for instance, whether they will be registered as a percent, a dollar amount, or a date. In order to adjust a number format, the user should first select the cell, row, or column that will be affected. Next, click Format, and then Number, to display the Format Cells dialog box. Once this dialog box is displayed, the user can type in the kind of formatting that he or she would like to implement. Works will provide an example of the selected style so that the user can confirm their selection. Then, he or she can click OK to apply this formatting style.

Changing Cell Alignment in a Works Spreadsheet

When working with a Works spreadsheet, you may want to adjust the horizontal or vertical alignment of the text or the numbers in certain cells. In order to do so, first select the cell, row, or column that you desire to format. Next, click Format, then Alignment, to call up the Alignment tab of the Format Cells dialog box. Next, select the desired horizontal and vertical positions within the cells. Unless adjustments are made, text will be flushed left and numbers will be flushed right. The user also may want to ensure that Works does not wrap any text values that do not fit on a single line; this can be done by unchecking Wrap Text within a Cell. Once the user is satisfied with his or her new alignments, clicking OK will apply the new formatting.

Changing Text Format in a Works Spreadsheet

Sometimes, a spreadsheet user wants to distinguish the contents of some cells, or create title headings for certain rows or columns. These functions can be performed by adjusting the text format. To do this, first select the cell, row, or column that is to be reformatted. Next, select the Format, and then hit the Font button to call up the Font tab of the Format Cells dialog box. Next, from the Select Font list, you can choose the appropriate font and style. At this point, you may also select the size of text, the color, and the presence of any underlining or striking-through. A newly created format can be made the automatic format by selecting the Set as Default button. Once you are satisfied with the text format, clicking OK applies it.

Formatting Borders in a Works Spreadsheet

Sometimes, when you want to draw attention to a certain cell, row, or column, it is a good idea to alter the borders that surround it. This can be easily done in Works by first selecting the area that you would like to format, and then clicking Format, then Border, to call up the Border tab of the Format Cells dialog box. Next, you can select the color of the border by picking one from a scrolling list. You may also adjust the line type, to make the line surrounding the border thicker or thinner as desired. By clicking the Border Location buttons, you can determine whether you would like a standard outline border, an inside grid, or no border at all. If you would like to design a border of your own, you can do this by adjusting the Border Location buttons; the results will be shown in a display window.

Adjusting Shading in a Works Spreadsheet

Some spreadsheet authors like to indicate the various sections of a spreadsheet by shading them variously. Adjusting the shading of a spreadsheet is quite simple. First, highlight whatever cell, row, or column you would like to adjust. Then, click Format, then Shading, to call up the Shading tab of the Format Cells dialog box. From this dialog box, you may select a color from a list, or choose Automatic to have Works select a contrasting color for you. You may then click on the color to create any pattern that you would like. Once you have decided on a color and pattern, and are satisfied with the look displayed in the Preview window, you may apply the shading by clicking OK.

Making calculations in a Works Spreadsheet

One of the most important applications of a spreadsheet is calculating values according to simple formulas. Formulas in Works will always begin with an equal sign; so, as a simple example, the formula to divide cell A1 by cell B1 would be =A1/B1. Because more complex formulas can be quite difficult to create, Works has included a helpful device called Easy Calc. To access Easy Calc, simply visit it in the menu under Tools or click the little calculator in the toolbar. Then, select the function you would like to have performed, and the cells that will be used in the calculation. Then, indicate where you would like the results of the calculation to be displayed. At this point, clicking on Finish will create the formula and enter it into the spreadsheet.

Adding a Chart to a Works Spreadsheet

Often, it is useful to create a visual representation of the data contained in your spreadsheet. In order to do this, first select the group of cells you would like to be included in the chart. Next, click Tools, and then Create New Chart, to display the New Chart dialog box. After that, you can click on the thumbnail that represents the kind of chart that you would like to create, and a Preview window will show you how your finished chart will look. Then, type a title for your chart and adjust the border by enabling the Show Border check box. By clicking on the Advanced Options tab, you may make any other fine-tunings you would like to your chart. Once you are finished, clicking OK creates and displays the chart.

Printing Spreadsheet Documents in Works

Many times, a spreadsheet author will want to have a hard copy of their document on file or for distribution to colleagues or students. It is always a good idea to click Print Preview under the File menu first, so that you can get an idea of what the document will look like once it has been printed. That way, you can go back and make adjustments if you are not satisfied. You can print from this screen, or you can click the Print icon on the toolbar or select the print option in the File menu. If you would like instead to send the spreadsheet to another person via email, you can do so by clicking File, then Send, and attaching the document to your message. This is a great way to save paper.

Reprographics

Reprographics is simply the reproduction of printed materials using high-speed printers and printing presses. Reprographic services may be needed by all businesses, but are especially necessary for those in the fields of construction, engineering, and architecture, in which large-scale plans may need to be reproduced many times with a high degree of clarity. Today, the top reprographic firms offer digital reproduction of fine art, digital photography reproduction, quick, massive commercial printing, and help with the construction of point-of-purchase displays. Moreover, reprographic firms help facilitate the transfer of reproduced documents by helping with delivery and logistics.

Processing Mail

Despite the growing popularity of electronic document transfer, there is still a great need for equipment for processing physical mail. Most businesses that handle a high volume of mail are likely to have a mail sorter and a mail opener. A mail sorter is programmed to separate mail into various departments, making it possible to expedite mail around the company. Businesses that have to send out a great deal of mail are likely to have a letter sealer, an automatic addresser for mass mailings, a postage machine, and postage scales. With these latter two devices, a business can measure and pay their own postage on large packages, and apply a sticker to the outgoing package indicating that postage has been paid.

Simulation Productivity

Recently, software has been developed that allows businesses to simulate their operations, and thereby get a better idea of what their productivity is likely to be and where they can make improvements. In simulation modeling, a small computer model is created using all the known elements of the operational system, at which point it is run so that the business managers can observe it. Simulation software is most commonly used to model manufacturing operations, since it is easy to predict all of the variables in a simple manufacturing task. However, system models are being increasingly implemented by other sectors of the economy, including the service industry. Many health care providers currently employ simulation software to help them achieve their productivity goals.

Computer Hardware

In the world of computers, hardware is any physical machinery or equipment. A computer requires both hardware and software to function. Hardware is distinguished by being physically tangible, and includes accessories like floppy disk drives, hard drives, CD-ROM drives, sound cards, video cards, modems, keyboards, mice, monitors, and printers. The quality of a computer's hardware affects how well its software can operate. Computers with larger hard drives, for instance, can store more information and handle more work. Computers with larger RAM can juggle more tasks simultaneously. A fast CPU allows the computer to process information and run programs more quickly. A business teacher should make sure that students are familiar with the basic types of computer hardware.

Computer Software

Computer software is the set of instructions delivered to the computer's hardware (the physical machinery of the computer) to accomplish certain tasks. A series of instructions that performs a particular task is known as a program. For most general types of computer users, there are three types of software. Platform software is the basic set of programs that allow a user to interact with the computer. This category includes operating systems, device drivers, and the basic input-output system. Application software is special task programs, like word processors or video games. Typically, application software must be purchased separately from a computer. User-written software includes things like spreadsheet templates, word-processing macros, and other small programs created by the user to speed up work.

Analog and Digital

Analog devices resemble in some way the thing that they represent. For example, an analog watch represents the motion of the planet by the revolution of a hand around some central axis; an analog telephone turns the vibrations of the human voice into electrical vibrations with a similar shape. For a long time, technology basically consisted of analog devices. In recent decades, however, there has been a trend towards digital devices. Digital equipment makes a numerical representation of the original: the time becomes a series of numbers rather than the motions of hands, and the human voice is encoded in a dense collection of numerical data. Digital information is much easier to process, record, and replicate.

Bits and Bytes in Computing

A bit, or binary digit, is the smallest unit of computer storage. It is either a one or a zero, the two elements that make up binary code. Physically, a bit is simply a transistor, a magnetic domain on a disk, a high or low voltage in a circuit, or a reflective spot on a compact disk. Bits are used as a measure of how much data a computer can process or transmit, or as a measure of the computer's memory capacity. When bits are referred to in this latter sense, they are usually described in terms of bytes, groups of eight bits. A byte, short for binary table, is meant to be the smallest unit of storage that can be considered by a computer. Business teachers should ensure that their students are up to date on the memory and processing speed requirements for all of the software that they are likely to need for work.

Peripheral Devices

A peripheral device is any component of a computer, excluding the motherboard, CPU, or working memory. Peripherals may include disks, monitors, keyboards, mice, printers, scanners, tape drives, microphones, speakers, cameras, and many other things. Peripherals are added to a computer to expand its capabilities. Typically, peripheral devices are seen as optional, although many would argue that a keyboard is necessary. Business teachers should be able to give their students some experience working with the more common peripherals, like scanners and tape drives. Most businesses use scanners for creating advertisements, among other things, and almost every business has some sort of back-up tape system to protect important information.

Floppy Disks and Hard Disks

Information may be stored on a computer on either a floppy or hard disk. A floppy disk is a reusable magnetic medium that is generally obsolete these days. Most businesses use CD-ROMs if they have a need for portable, tangible data storage media. For the most part, though, businesses rely on their hard disk drives for data storage. Hard disk drives are made of aluminum or glass platter coated with a magnetic material, on which large amounts of data can be stored. It is much faster to retrieve information from hard disk drives than from floppy disks. In the past decade, the size and speed of hard drives has improved to the point that, along with the easy file transferability made possible by the Internet, they have essentially made floppy disks unnecessary.

Modems

A modem is a computer device that sends information, usually digital data, over a network connection. The word *modem* is a combination of the words *modulator* and *demodulator*. Older, analog modems take digital data and convert them into audio tones that can be transferred over a telephone line. More common these days are cable and DSL modems, which use different means to transmit a greater amount of data at a higher speed. Cable modems connect with the Internet through an Ethernet port, which has a much greater bandwidth than a normal telephone port. DSL (digital subscriber line) modems are tailored to download information extremely quickly, although they may be slow in uploading.

Bandwidth

When Internet experts discuss bandwidth, they mean the amount of data that a system can transmit at a given time. High bandwidth means that a computer can transmit data very quickly, or can transmit multiple streams of data at the same time. Typically, bandwidth is only as good as the weakest link in the network chain. In digital systems, bandwidth is typically measured in bits per second (bps). The term *bandwidth* should not lead one to assume that it only applies to systems connected to the Internet by a cable; bandwidth also applies to wireless connections.

Serial Ports, Parallel Ports, and USB Ports

A serial port is a socket on a computer used to transfer data one bit at a time. Serial ports have been used to connect modems, mice, printers, keyboards, and other external devices to a computer. The serial port has recently been overshadowed, however, by parallel and USB ports. Parallel ports operate in a similar manner to serial ports, with the exception that they can transfer eight bits (one byte) of data at a time. Most current computers have at least one parallel port for a printer, scanner, or other external device. Increasingly popular, however, are USB (universal serial bus) ports, which can transfer 12 megabytes of data every second. They are quickly becoming the standard way of connecting printers and modems to a computer.

Digital Cameras

A digital camera transmits pictures directly to a computer or records them onto a disk without using film. Digital cameras have largely overtaken regular cameras as the preferred way to perform basic photographic functions. The main consideration regarding digital cameras is the number of pixels contained in the image (a pixel is a graphical dot that makes up an image). The image on a TV screen is about 400 x 600 pixels, whereas a good 35mm slide is about 2000 x 3000 pixels. A digital camera generally falls somewhere in between these two. A digital camera can usually store hundreds of images at a time, which can be transferred to a computer via a USB port. Digital images can also be previewed on an LCD screen found on the back of most digital cameras.

Intranet and TCP/IP

An intranet is any network that functions in a manner similar to the Internet, but is restricted to a certain pool of users. Intranets may or may not be connected to the Internet at large. These smaller networks are extremely popular in business; companies frequently use them to set up channels for distributing information throughout their organization. This is possible both because inexpensive servers have become available in recent years, and because the development of TCP/IP software has made it possible to set up networks easily. TCP/IP is a communications protocol that establishes a standard mode of address, allowing different computers to interact with one another. TCP/IP stands for transmission control protocol/ Internet protocol.

ROM

ROM stands for read-only memory. This, as the name indicates, is memory on a computer that can be read but not altered. A computer will hold onto information stored in ROM even when the power is turned off. The user or the computer manufacturer only needs to place information in ROM one time; it will remain there forever. For this reason, ROM memory space is mainly used for the storage of the most essential programs for running the computer, those which are unlikely to require frequent updating. At present, most ROMs look much like random access memory (RAM) chips. Although ROM is increasingly becoming obsolete in favor of external storage devices, many computers, video-game systems, and other computer-based technologies still rely on ROM to maintain important data.

RAM

RAM stands for random access memory. It is pronounced in the same way as the name for a male sheep. A computer's RAM is composed of small memory chips linked to the motherboard of the computer. Whenever a computer user accesses a particular program from the hard drive, it is moved from the hard drive to the RAM, as it is much faster for a computer to read data from RAM than from the permanent hard drive. It makes sense, then, that the more RAM a computer has, the more large and complex programs it will be able to run at the same time. RAM can be thought of as a sort of short-term memory; if your computer can perform a number of tasks at the same time, it will be able to function more effectively. Many experts say that adding RAM to a computer is better than improving CPU.

CD-ROMs

CD-ROM stands for compact disc- read-only memory. This is a data storage format wherein text, graphics, and audio files can be stored on a plastic disc. CD-ROMs use a different format for recording data than do audio CDs. Most computers have a CD-ROM connected to the motherboard. CD-ROMs can hold 650 MB of data, which is about the same as 250,000 pages of text. The data is encoded at microscopic size, which is why so much can be placed on each disc. The data is recorded in binary code as a series of bumps entered onto the surface of the plastic disc; a laser then "reads" these bumps through reflection and transmits the data. There are a great number of business programs and simulations available in CD-ROM format.

CPU

CPU stands for central processing unit. Put simply, it is the part of a computer that actually does the "computing." Most computers have their entire CPU stored on a single chip. A CPU's operation consists of the actions of its two main components: the control unit and the various execution units. A control unit is the circuitry that finds and analyzes each instruction in a certain program. The execution units are those that perform the tasks in a program. Although many computer dealers mistakenly call the entire computer case on a desktop computer the CPU, it is actually only that part of the computer which performs the tasks of adding, subtracting, moving, retrieving, and so on. The rest of the space in a desktop computer's tower is devoted to memory, disc drives, and various other hardware.

LAN and Ethernet

The acronym LAN stands for Local Area Network, and is pronounced like "land" without the "d." A LAN is any small computer network, typically one that is restricted to a certain building, office, university, or home. Most businesses have their own LAN, which enables their employees to share information more easily. These are most often Ethernet connections, meaning that they connect through a port on the computer that looks like a phone jack, except slightly wider. An Ethernet port can be used to connect a computer to another computer, to a LAN network, or simply to an external modem. Ethernet connections are able to transfer data much more quickly than connections that use a regular telephone jack. However, many companies are now getting rid of Ethernet-based LANs in favor of wireless networks.

Parts of an Internet Address (URL)

Individuals may access content on the Internet by typing the appropriate URL into the location bar. A URL, or uniform resource locator, is the web page's address, and has a few different parts. Let us take as an example the URL http://www.example.com. Here, the "http:" signifies the protocol used to read this page. In this case, it is the HyperText Transfer Protocol. The "www" stands for World Wide Web, and is the name of the host computer on which the data is stored. Most computers that are hooked up to the Internet simply have "www" here, although they need not. The next bit, "example.com," is the domain name, indicating that the page "example" is coming from a commercial site. Other domain designators are "edu" for education, "org" for organization, and "gov" for government sites.

Internet Browsers, Bookmarks, and Servers

In the context of the Internet, a browser is a program that mediates content for a computer user. In order to visit a particular Internet site, one simply types its address into the browser's location field. Most browsers have a home page that serves as an index to the various sites on the Internet. Most browsers allow the user to create bookmarks, immediate links to their favorite sites on the Internet. An Internet server is a computer that is connected to a network and used by multiple individuals. Individuals who wish to run web pages allow their computers to be servers for that page; other computers that are connected to the network can access the web page by briefly accessing the server computer.

Bandwidth, Cache, CGI, Cookies, and IP Address

In the context of the Internet, bandwidth is the measurement of how quickly data can be passed from one computer to another. It may be measured either in Kilobits per second (Kbps) or Megabits per second (Mbps). A cache is a place, either on one's computer or on computers operated by one's service provider, where copies of previously accessed web pages are stored so that they may be quickly brought up again. The Common Gateway Interface (CGI) is the set of rules that allows an Internet browser to interact with a program on the web server. Cookies are small text files that a user downloads to his or her computer, and which may be used to track the user's behavior or to allow for customized browsing. An Internet Protocol (IP) address is a computer's numerical tag, which identifies it on the Internet.

Domain Names, FTP, Firewalls, and HTML

On the Internet, a domain name is simply a unique title that distinguishes one or more IP addresses. Domain names are used for sending e-mail and as addresses for web pages. File Transfer Protocol (FTP) is a means of transferring files from one computer to another over the Internet. Although FTP is the most popular means of transferring files, it is not entirely safe; passwords and file contents may be intercepted. A firewall is any software or hardware that monitors and controls the information moving in and out of a computer network. Firewalls are meant to protect computers from being accessed by unauthorized users. HyperText Markup Language (HTML) is the basic language of the Internet; every web page is written in this language, which uses simple tags to divide sections of documents.

HTTP, ISP, Mark-up, Plug-in, and Servers

HyperText Transfer Protocol (HTTP) is the most common example of the procedure computers use to communicate on the Internet. An Internet Service Provider (ISP) is an organization that enables users to access the Internet. Typically, users are charged for this privilege. Mark-up is the process through which documents are turned into web pages by inserting HTML tags. On the Internet, a plug-in is a program that enables a computer to access a broader array of content. Common plug-ins allow computers to access certain kinds of video and audio files. A server is a computer on the Internet that provides information for other computers. Servers might enable other users to view web pages or send email.

Cybersquatting

As the Internet has become a more viable arena for business, certain questionable business practices have evolved as well. Cybersquatting is registering a domain name with the express purpose of reselling it later for a profit. In these cases, the individual selects a domain name that they anticipate will become desired either because of its similarity to a familiar brand or its connection to an area of business. In 1999, the United States passed the Anti-Cybersquatting Consumer Protection Act, which allows trademark-holders to receive damages from cybersquatters who have registered trade names or similar names in an attempt to extort money from the business. This law has not entirely eliminated the practice of cybersquatting, but it has made it more difficult to do successfully.

Internet Page Hijacking

Now that the Internet has become the venue for so much American business, it is important for business teachers to teach their students about the various scams there. The phrase page hijacking refers to a host of dirty tricks, most of which result in a surfer being directed to a web page that he or she had not intended to visit. One common means of doing this is to change the user's home page in his or her default settings, thereby causing the user to visit some other site every time he or she starts up the browser. Page hijacking may also refer to the practice of copying Internet content from one page to another, so that search engines will refer users to the second page, on which the hijacker then enters other information.

Internet Phishing

Phishing is one of the many forms of Internet scamming that has cropped up as more business is transacted on-line. Specifically, phishing is a form of identity theft in which a website claims to represent a legitimate business, but actually is a front so that criminals can acquire personal data from would-be buyers. Some of the more successful phishers have set up web pages that look like those of a major bank, then sent emails from that site to account holders asking for personal information. If the individuals are foolish enough to provide the information, the scammer can then access their bank accounts. Some phishers are sophisticated enough to change the programming code underlying a business' website so that visitors are redirected to a fake site, with neither the business nor the visitor ever knowing.

Normal Post Mail

The employees of an office will have to use a number of different forms of mail, depending on their purpose. Many professionals still use the United States Postal Service, otherwise known as "snail mail," because it is reliable and retains an air of authority. Professionals can also use the special delivery services offered by the Postal Service and by various private delivery services. It is now possible for businesses to create a shipping order on-line and have the document or package picked up at their office. Typically, the length of time it will take to have the item delivered is guaranteed in the terms of the order. These methods are still very popular in business despite the growing presence of electronic mail.

Fax and Email

Although the fax machine has been somewhat replaced by Internet technology in the past few years, most businesses maintain fax service and use it often. Faxes are valued for speed and immediate confirmation of delivery, meaning that there is no anxiety over whether the document has arrived intact. Faxes require a cover sheet listing the date, recipient, sender, and total number of pages. E-mail is probably the most popular form of office mail these days. Although it is still seen as somewhat informal, the speed and ease of electronic mail makes it very popular in the business world. One can also attach a more formal document (for instance a word-processing document, a database, or a spreadsheet) to an email message to create a more formal appearance.

Macros

A macro enables a computer user to perform with one keystroke a commonly-performed command that would normally take several keystrokes. Word processing programs often allow the use of macros for editing and formatting. Many users also create macros to insert common elements into their documents, for instance tables of a certain size or configuration. Typically, word processing programs have a recorder so that users can enter the commands which they want the macro to accomplish, and then decide which keystroke will accomplish this action. Users of some programs can create a space for macros on the toolbar, so that they can be enacted with the click of a button.

Mailing Documents

Despite the growing popularity of electronic data transfer, companies still need to send documents and other items through the regular postal service. In order to make their service more attractive to the modern business community, the federal Postal Service and various private delivery businesses have made many shipping tasks available on-line. Customers can create shipping orders, print out the appropriate bar codes, and select the shipping speed with the click of a mouse. Most large businesses have sophisticated equipment for printing out bar code stickers.

Programs and Professional Development

Career Clusters

In this extremely specialized modern economy, it is useful to consider various "clusters" of careers with similar attributes. The United States government has established sixteen career clusters: agriculture and natural resources; arts/audio/video technology and communications; architecture and construction; business and administration; education and training; finance; government and public administration; health science; hospitality and tourism; human services; information technology services; law and public safety; manufacturing; retail/wholesale sales and services; scientific research and engineering; and transportation distribution and logistics. These clusters have been created in part to aid vocational educators, who may be overwhelmed by the variety of potential careers and can benefit from a system of summary.

How Career Clusters Determine Job Aptitude

One of the main uses of the system of career clusters as devised by the United States government is to provide vocational educators with a simplified way of looking at the skills and standards required for various types of jobs. The government has developed extensive paperwork regarding each of the sixteen skill sets, complete with specific training and skills required. Oftentimes, vocational teachers will administer a questionnaire to determine which career clusters best suit the interests and aptitudes of the students. Then, with the help of the available literature, the teacher can work with the student to develop a plan for attaining the skills necessary for employment in their chosen field.

Work Standards for Employees

It is very important that an employer enforce clear standards for employees. In order to do this successfully, the employer needs to make sure that standards are posted visibly and that employees are introduced to them during orientation. Employers should set a good example by following all the rules themselves. Employers should demonstrate to their subordinates that the business prizes accuracy and honesty. Finally, a good way to ensure that employee work standards will be attained is to set performance goals and reward employees for reaching them. Work standards may have to do with customer service, accuracy in bookkeeping, cleanliness, punctuality, productivity, or safety.

How to Improve Employee Attitudes

Some business analysts note a mismatch between the passion for personal liberty in the United States and the authoritarian hierarchies of American business. Over the course of the twentieth century, statistics have demonstrated a gradual decrease in the trust American workers have in their employers. At the same time, the average age of American workers and management has decreased, so there is reason to suspect that communication between employer and employee may improve. One means of increasing employee satisfaction is through the formation of quality circles, groups of people that meet to discuss work-related issues. Many statistics show that workers are now more concerned with being challenged and feeling important than with earning money to survive; the modern manager will have to do more than pay his employees to make them feel satisfied.

Peer Relationships at Work

Solid relationships among employees must be maintained if productivity is to be maximized. Oftentimes, intensely focused individuals can actually undermine an organization by alienating their coworkers and inhibiting the flow of knowledge throughout the company. As a manager, it is crucial to monitor the relationships among staff and ensure that positive communication is taking place. Many businesses devote time to building relationships: they feel that taking a bit of time away from work to develop trust and friendship in the company will lead to greater productivity in the long run.

Building Strong Relationships Among Staff

There are a few easy ways for managers to develop positive working relationships among the members of their staff. One way is to set aside some time for company lunches or outings, so that fellow employees can get to know one another personally. Passing on compliments and bestowing praise on positive behavior is another way to nurture a good work environment. If a manager wants to encourage communication among his or her employees, then he or she should set a good example by keeping the staff informed and involved in the managerial operations. Most importantly, a manager should always be a good listener, so that employees will get the impression that their ideas are valued and appreciated.

Selection and Recruiting of Personnel

Effective human resources managers do a great deal of preliminary work before selecting employees. They must have a good description of organizational needs and necessary qualifications. It is also important for a business to have a standardized method of selection. If there is no standard procedure for hiring, a manager is likely to make one of three mistakes. The first mistake is not planning for potential future problems. Another common mistake is assuming that the right employees will be available when they are needed. The last common mistake is trusting personal judgment to an inordinate degree. Companies may require resumes and psychological exams, but then ignore this collected information to follow some personal intuition. Rather than doing this, managers should have a clear idea of their selection needs and process.

Nondiscriminatory Discrimination

Screening is always the first part of the recruiting process. Some companies have recruiting officers who travel to universities to interview potential employees. In any case, it is important that the firm have a good set of minimum requirements, and that they do not bother to interview everyone who is interested in a job. An able recruiter should establish close relationships with people at the place of recruiting, so that he or she will have an available reference for candidates. Usually, resumes are used to screen candidates at first. Business analysts agree that it is best for a company to have an immediate idea of a candidate's weaknesses; being placed in a job for which one is unqualified is as bad for the employee as it is for the company.

Civil Rights Act of 1964 and the EEOC

The United States government has established laws to ensure that all citizens are given a fair chance at available jobs. The Civil Rights Act of 1964 decreed that it is illegal to discriminate against candidates because of their race, ethnicity, religion, or gender. Title VII of this act established the Equal Employment Opportunity Commission (EEOC), which seems to increase job opportunities for women and minorities. Since its inception, the EEOC has been enhanced by the Equal Pay Act of 1963, the Age Discrimination in Employment Act of 1967, and the Equal Employment Opportunity Act of 1972. These laws apply to business, state and local governments, labor unions, and educational institutions.

How to Write a Good Job Description

In order to attract appropriate candidates for an available position in his or her business, a manager has to be able to write a clear and precise job description. A good job description is similar to a job contract: it outlines what the employer wants, and indicates what the employee will get in return. It should include a description of the physical tasks of the job, the training that will be provided, the authority and responsibility of the job, the goals and objectives of the job, and a brief account of the payment offered. In a medium to large business, it is always a good idea for the manager to show the completed job description to the employees who know the most about the available job, to make sure that they concur.

Application Forms in the Hiring Procedure

Large businesses can be overwhelmed by the volume of resumes that they receive, even when they are not advertising vacancies. For this reason, it often makes sense for them to compose a standard application form for every prospective employee to fill out. This allows the business to inquire directly about the things that are important to them, rather than allow candidates to mention anything they believe to be significant. By law, application forms cannot inquire about age, marital status, arrest records, gender, religion, citizenship, or nationality. All of these things are considered to be possible sources of discrimination in hiring. Application forms should be concise and clear, so that managers can look through a large number of them quickly.

Internal Candidates in the Hiring Procedure

If at all possible, managers should try to promote individuals from within the company to fill upper-level vacancies. There are a number of reasons for doing so. First, it is good for company morale to see an employee rewarded for his or her good work; internal promotion gives the impression that hard work will be acknowledged. Moreover, internal candidates already know the basic structure and workings of the organization and will therefore require less orientation and training. In order to give current employees the best possible chance to fill a vacancy, managers should advertise job descriptions in the company newsletter and mention vacancies at company gatherings.

External Candidates in the Hiring Process

In some cases, especially for newly-created positions, it will be appropriate to search exclusively outside the company for new employees. There are a number of ways to do this. The most common way to attract external candidates is to advertise in the print media. This approach often results in an overabundance of unqualified applicants; however, so many businesses have taken to using headhunters, people who have made a career out of matching individuals with companies. Employment and staffing agencies are also good ways for a business to fill their vacancies with minimal stress. Perhaps the best way for a manager to discover great job candidates is simply by asking around in his or her business network.

Conducting a Job Interview

Learning how to conduct a proper job interview takes experience. However, there a few fundamental tips that a manager should know before meeting with prospective employees. First, be prepared. Unless interview questions are planned, an inexperienced manager will not be able to use the time to get to know the candidate. Instead, he or she will be occupied trying to remember what questions to ask. Besides any specific information to be obtained, the job interview should give the manager a general sense of the candidate's character, confidence, and intelligence. A well-structured interview allows a manager to focus on developing an overall impression of the candidate, and enables the manager to pursue interesting subjects at his or her discretion.

Key Interview Questions

The questions that are appropriate for a job interview will depend on the job; a manager needs to ensure that the candidate has whatever skills and training are required. Still, there are some general questions that are appropriate for just about any interview. For instance, most managers like to ask candidates why they are interested in a job, or where they first learned about the vacancy. These questions give the candidate a chance to speak at length about his or her interests and goals. It is important for a manager to ask questions that require more than a simple "yes or "no," so that he or she can get an idea of how the candidate's mind works. Asking for opinions, or for a description of some past experience, is a good way to draw out the applicant's personality.

Checking References and Administering Tests

Although checking references is not always a fun experience, it is an invaluable tool for learning more about job applicants. Most managers are astonished by the honest information they can find out about potential employees just by calling up their previous employers. Even if the company finds its applicants through a headhunter or employment agency, it is a good idea to check with the applicant's references. Companies may also find it helpful to administer psychological, medical, IQ, or dexterity tests to their applicants. It is a good idea to limit testing to those areas that are directly relevant to the position offered; dexterity testing for a receptionist position, for example, might be unnecessary. Drug testing is also frequently administered by businesses, although it is illegal in some cases.

Offer Sheets

Once a manager has decided to offer employment to a particular candidate, the next step in the hiring process is to design an offer sheet. An offer sheet should include the job description and title, the starting date, the starting salary, a summary of the compensation package, a copy of the business' organizational chart, and a deadline for acceptance or refusal of the offer. It is not rare for a first job offer to be refused. Still, managers should always make sure that their payment offers are consistent with the company's pay scale, to avoid jealousy within the company. Also, it is a good idea to hire new employees on a three-month probationary basis. Finally, managers should avoid drawing up employment contracts, unless it is very important to prevent employees from working for a competitor for any length of time.

Salary Negotiation

After appraising all the objective data about a particular candidate, managers will typically determine whether they can agree with him or her on a potential salary. It is best for managers not to spend too much time touting the good qualities of the business; oversold employees may easily become embittered. Typically, hiring decisions regarding low-level employees can be made fairly quickly. More time will be taken to fill managerial vacancies, and there will usually be a series of interviews to accompany whatever battery of tests is administered to potential employees. Many companies have established their own selection formulas, composed of a blend of psychological tests, interviews, and charts.

Employee Orientation

Orientation is the introduction of new employees into the culture of the company. Most businesses will include a partial orientation in the hiring process, so that employees can determine whether the job is a good fit. Once hired, though, employees will receive a full orientation, which usually includes the following: company history and major operations; general company policies and rules; outline of the organizational structure; rules concerning wages, overtime, vacations, and holidays; the available economic and recreational services, such as insurance or pensions; the system for promotion and transfer; and the procedures for filing a complaint or making a suggestion.

Informal Means of Employee Orientation

Of course, new employees will not remember everything they are told during a formal orientation. There are several other ways for them to become experienced on the job. In vestibule training, new employees are led through a brief course of training in an environment identical to the one in which they will work. This method of orientation is often used by factories. In on-the-job training, the new employee learns his or her job by performing it. Apprenticeship is a common form of orientation in skilled jobs: here, the new employee is mentored by a veteran employee with long experience in the field. In management positions, orientation may take the form of job rotation, in which employees receive training in several different fields. "Assistant-to" positions give new employees a chance to tag along with some senior executive and thereby get a feel for the job.

Business Standards

The standards in a business are the areas in which performance is assessed. An airline, for example, might establish standards in sales, customer service, or repair quality. Clear and verifiable standards are important, since managers cannot oversee every aspect of operations; employees need to have some consistent idea of the company's expectations for them. Effective managers will only set a few important standards for their employees, so that these can be given enough attention. For this reason, it is essential that managers select the few standards that will give them the best indication that their subordinates are doing their jobs well. Performance may be measured in money, quotas, time, speed, quality, or volume.

Basic Performance Appraisals

Every business needs some way to assess the competence and efficiency of its employees. Although it is almost universally unpopular, performance appraisal is necessary in every field. From the point of view of management, the purpose of performance appraisal is to properly allocate resources, to reestablish focus on the company's goals, and to give employees a venue to express their feelings about their job and the company. Oftentimes, the performance appraisal process is more remarkable for what it reveals about the business than for what it says about any particular employee. Some managers dislike performance appraisal because they fail to understand it as a chance to improve the business; nevertheless, it is essential that appraisal systems be clear and precise, so that a company can continue to get the maximum from satisfied employees.

Including Company History in a Performance Appraisal

It seems absurd, but many managers continue to assess company progress without comparing the present data with the data of the past. In order to really understand how a business is developing, it is crucial to compare the accounting numbers from year to year. Some companies even begin their budgeting for the next year by entering all the data from the previous year and then making adjustments. While this method may work best for businesses with consistent operations, every business should revisit their numbers from previous years during performance appraisal. This is one way to ensure that appraisal is conducted objectively and fairly.

Benchmarking and Performance Appraisal

One way that many businesses assess their performance is by comparing themselves with the best businesses in their field and in the economy in general. This process, known as benchmarking, is effective if it inspires employees to make specific beneficial changes. Managers should avoid, however, setting standards for their business that are unreachable and may become discouraging. In order for benchmarking to be useful, a business should make very specific comparisons, like between customer service departments or between specific accounts. Many businesses motivate themselves by competing for the Baldridge Award, a prize given out every year to the American companies with the best marks for quality control.

Employee Pay

Large corporations use a variety of measures to determine the rate of employee pay. Wages are the employee's pay based on hours of work or the specific units of completed work. A salary, on the other hand, is pay based on time at work (when that time is measured in weeks, months, or years). Salaries are generally paid on a weekly, semi-monthly, or monthly basis, and are typically reserved for managerial positions. A guaranteed annual wage (GAW) is the number of hours of work in a year that a company promises its employees. A GAW may be important in businesses that tend to have varying production demands throughout the year. A bonus is anything awarded to an employee for special performance, especially when the money is derived from profits.

Overtime pay, Incentive pay, Profit Sharing, Insurance, and Paid Vacation

Overtime pay is usually one and one-half times the normal wage, and is paid for hours worked in excess of the normal amount. Usually, salaried employees are exempt from overtime pay. Incentive pay is given to employees as a reward for meeting certain production goals; it is usually offered to stimulate increased productivity. Profit sharing is any system whereby employees are entitled to a certain amount of the company's profits, whether in cash or as contributions to their pension plans. Insurance, in this context, is any group, life, health, or disability insurance paid for by the company. Paid vacations, of course, are time off from work in which the employee continues to receive full pay.

Stock Options, Savings Plans, Retirement/Pension Plans, and Additional Non-Money Benefits

Stock options are chances for employees to purchase company stock for a period of five or ten years, at prices set when the option is awarded. Obviously, employees hope that the price of the stock will go up after the stock options are handed out. A savings plan is a savings account or pension plan sponsored by a company. Often, employers will put money in the account proportional to the amount that the employee deposits. A retirement or pension plan is a company's provision for the retirement of the employee. It is usually based on length of service and pay level. These plans are given in addition to Social Security benefits, and are often financed by company profits. Besides all these forms of compensation, employees may also receive discounts on company products, special gifts at the holidays, or military leaves of absence.

Promotion

The most common path to higher compensation is advancement to a higher position in the company, otherwise known as promotion. Of course, there are social and psychological advantages to promotion besides the increase in pay. Companies have various means of determining when employees will be promoted or given a raise. Some companies use a merit-rating system, in which every employee is evaluated at a certain interval. Employees are assessed for their dependability, initiative, handling of responsibility, appearance, production, use of resources, and the amount of supervision they require. If an employee seems to have demonstrated positive progress in these areas, he or she will receive a raise or promotion. Some critics of this system suggest that it tends to degenerate into a system of automatic rewards, without the accompanying evaluation.

Seniority System

When union members are allowed to vote on their company's system for promotions and raises, they almost always select the seniority system, in which decisions regarding advancement and elimination of employees are made based on the employee's length of service. Of course, this system does not always work in the best interests of the company; those employees who have been around the longest may not be the most qualified for advancement. However, a seniority system may seem like an objective alternative to a merit-based system of promotion, which can be perceived as unfair or prejudiced. The seniority system also tends to induce complacency among employees, who may feel that they can just wait for their inevitable promotion.

The Peter Principle

The Peter Principle is a somewhat satirical notion about the way promotions work in a bureaucratic organization. It stems from a common mistake made by managers: namely, assuming that because an employee can do one thing well, they will be able to do another, more complicated thing well also. The Peter Principle asserts that individuals who are competent at their work will be promoted again and again, until they eventually reach a position for which they are not qualified. At this point, the organization will have damaged itself, by removing a worker from a position of competence and placing him or her in a position of incompetence. Frequently, the drive for more money and higher status propels workers into jobs for which they are simply not qualified.

Personnel Termination

Employee termination can take a number of different forms. Many workers are considered terminated when they retire. For the purposes of the company, the money an individual receives after retiring was earned during the period of service, and was simply deferred until the employee became inactive. Retirement plans are influenced by the state of the economy, rate of unemployment, life expectancy, and rate of inflation. Another kind of termination occurs when workers voluntarily leave a company to work somewhere else. In the American business community, mobility is much greater than in countries (like Japan) where loyalty to an employer is more carefully cultivated. Employee termination can also take the form of layoffs, whether motivated by poor performance or by declines in the industry.

Resume

Resume composition
A resume may be the most important document that students will ever compose in their lives, so it is essential that business teachers give them the skills to construct thoughtful and effective ones. It is essential first of all that students have an idea of who the target audience is for their resume. If they are applying for a babysitting job, for instance, they should highlight different aspects of their background than if they were applying for an internship with their local congressman. A student should think of the resume as a marketing tool, in which the product being sold is him or herself. To this end, a resume should make clear the unique and positive attributes of the student, without going into too much detail. After all, a resume aims to earn an interview, not necessarily a job. Too many resumes are overloaded with accomplishments, to the point where they are either unbelievable or unreadable.

Grammar and style in resume composition
There are a few stylistic points that students should keep in mind when they are composing a resume. First, they should always use short, bulleted statements rather than lengthy descriptions. After all, they can expect that their potential employer is going to be looking over a large number of resumes, and so they need to make the information immediately accessible. A resume should try to use as many action words as possible, rather than using forms of "to be" or passive verbs. If the student is applying for a job in a particular field, it may help to demonstrate some knowledge of the terminology associated with that field, as

well as to mention any experience with the kind of work that will be required. Finally, and most obviously, a resume must contain no grammatical or spelling errors!

Looking forward when composing a resume

One of the quirky things about writing a resume is that, even though it lists your past achievements, it is actually supposed to be a document about your future. That is, an effective resume should suggest your ability to do the desired job, rather than show your past successes in their best light. So, the accomplishments that you list should be those that will be the most impressive to your desired employer, not those that you happen to think are noteworthy. A good resume should always lead off with a statement of purpose, so that whoever reads it knows immediately what you would like to be doing. Then, you should design the rest of the resume as if it were an advertisement for yourself, showing how you can fill the role you desire.

Avoiding overabundance in resume composition

Some students will have been a part of many organizations, received many awards, and therefore have a number of things to list on a resume. However, they should be discouraged from including everything. A proper resume will take its cues from its statement of purpose; in other words, if a certain achievement doesn't support your desire to do the work you are aiming for, it has no place on your resume. Including too much information will only confuse whoever reads the resume, and may result in that person not reading it any further. This may be of particular concern if you are applying for a job for which you feel overqualified. Many times, individuals in desperate need of a job apply for positions that are below their level of training. They may feel concerned that their full resume will put off potential employers; it is perfectly acceptable in such a case to omit certain data, as long as the resume remains truthful and doesn't contain any large gaps in the employment history.

Job descriptions on a resume

Too often, resumes include long, detailed descriptions of the duties and responsibilities the applicant held at a previous job. For the most part, these summaries should be avoided in favor of lists of job achievements. The main reason for this is that a simple job description does not convey to the resume reader that the applicant is particularly good at his or her job; in many cases, it may simply tell the reader things about a certain job that he or she already knew or could have guessed. It is much better to alert the reader to whatever success you may have had in a previous position, or to indicate any special privileges or duties that would not normally be considered part of the job.

Excluding irrelevant information from a resume

In order for a resume to net the desired job, it must be oriented to promote the idea that you are capable of that job. In other words, you should avoid bragging about skills you no longer wish to use, or describing jobs you no longer wish to perform. Say, for instance, that you had a managerial job in a restaurant in which you were frequently called upon to wash dishes; it would be foolish to apply for another managerial position by mentioning how great your dish-washing skills are. This is not to say that one should lie about one's job history, but simply that one should only advertise what one has an interest in providing to a future employer. Nondisclosure (that is, not mentioning something) is not the same thing as lying.

Lying on a resume

One of the most important things a student can learn about composing a resume is the stupidity of lying. Resume lies can take a number of forms, from misrepresenting your duties and position at a former job to claiming degrees you haven't obtained. No form of misrepresentation is acceptable on a resume; besides being immoral, it is bound to catch up with you. The advent of high-powered search engines has made it quite easy for companies to check up on the claims of their applicants, and any candidate who lies on their resume can be assured that if it is discovered during the selection process he will be disqualified, and if it is discovered after he has been hired he will most likely be terminated.

Job objectives on a resume

Every resume should begin with a job objective. The job objective sets the tone for the rest of the resume by answering three key questions: what position you are seeking to find, who should be reading your application materials, and how to interpret your resume. In order for this to work, of course, a job objective must be clear and precise. You should not say something like, "I want to improve myself and work as part of a cohesive team." Of course this may be true, but a potential employer needs to hear exactly what you want to do for his or her company, so that he or she can start visualizing you in that position as he or she reads the rest of the resume. A strong objective, with action verbs and precise terminology, immediately separates a quality resume from the pack.

Summary of qualifications on a resume

After a job objective is given, an effective resume will provide a brief summary of qualifications; that is, a list of the three or four best reasons for you to be considered for the job. This is the place to mention whatever you consider to be your most impressive, and most relevant, attribute. This might include your experience, credentials, special expertise, work ethic, or personality. Note that a summary of qualifications does not have to reference specific achievements. This is not to say, however, that it should be general. On the contrary, you should take this opportunity to highlight the skills that make you different from every other applicant, and therefore worthy of special consideration.

Work history on a resume

The work history section of a resume is your opportunity to showcase whatever experience and training you have already acquired, so long as it is pertinent to the job for which you are applying. Even if a job you have had is not directly relevant to your desired job, however, it is a good idea to briefly list it so as to avoid giving the impression that you have been unemployed for long periods. If there are gaps in your employment record, it is a good idea to indicate that you were not just lying about during this period by entering something like "student" or "personal travel," and then giving a brief summary. Job candidates should avoid mentioning rehabilitation, unemployment, or personal illness unless it is absolutely necessary.

Promotions and job changes on a resume

If you have been promoted at a past job, the work history section of your resume is the right place to indicate it. Future employers will naturally be impressed by candidates who have apparently thrived in their past jobs. In order to effectively show these promotions, you can create separate entries for each position you have held—just make sure to list the name of the company for each, so that readers won't think you simply changed employers often. If in fact you have worked for a number of companies over a brief period of time, however, you should try to minimize the impression of flightiness this might give by simply listing the employment agency you were working with, or indicating that you were performing strictly contractual work by including a title like "consultant" or "contractor."

Listing achievements on a resume

Every resume should include a list of achievements that indicate particular skills relevant to the job or general personal qualities that will be appreciated in an employee. In fact, a successful resume will frame every job description in terms of achievements; that is, instead of describing the responsibilities held and tasks performed, a good resume will list the skills acquired and advances made. The ideas that you are trying to convey by listing achievements are that you have the skills to do the job, you are proud of these skills, and you hope to continue using them in the future. For this reason, it is a good idea to downplay any achievements that may seem irrelevant to the job for which you are applying, and especially those which may make it seem as if you are overqualified.

Creating a cover letter

In order for a letter of application (or cover letter) to have the desired effect, it must be tailored to its audience. This means finding out the name and title of the person who will read the letter, even if this requires a bit of research. A proper cover letter should also give the reader a bit of insight into the author; including some personal experience or anecdote is a good way to distinguish one's letter from the rest. In this line, it is important to try and disguise whatever letter form the author may be using. Many applicants are helped by using available templates for application letters, but it should never be apparent to the reader that a cover letter "formula" is being used. A cover letter should always strive to represent the individuality of the person it represents.

How a resume catches the reader's attention

Since business managers will read many letters of application, business students need some strategies to help their letters stand out from the pack. The most important place to distinguish oneself is in the opening paragraph. Rather than use some formulaic introduction, a student should pique the reader's interest with an anecdote, or a clever way of mentioning how the job came to his or her attention. Certainly, a letter of application should stay on message, but too many students damage their chances for employment by merely filling in the blanks of some cover letter model. Instead of doing this, the savvy applicant will indirectly demonstrate his or her intelligence and familiarity with the company without boring the reader with empty praise or false modesty.

Letter of Application

There are a few essential tips that concern the composition of all letters of application, and that any business class should be sure to impart to students. First, a cover letter should always refer the reader to the application, or to any other documents contained in the same envelope. A cover letter should always end with a clear and courteous offer for an interview, and should of course include the same contact information as the resume. It goes without saying that any letters of application should be scrutinized closely for spelling and grammatical errors. An accomplished cover letter will be professional without being boring, and interesting without being too casual. Students should always have a friend or mentor read their cover letters before submitting it.

Job Interview

Preparation

In order to be fully prepared for a job interview, a candidate must have considered three areas. First, the candidate must have a general understanding of her own skills, strengths, and weaknesses. This is essential so that she can decide whether the job is truly appropriate for her. Next, the candidate must have prepared for the questions she is likely to be asked, both those that are standard to a job interview (for instance, why she would like the job, or what she already knows about the company) and those that are unique to the company. So that these last questions may be answered effectively, the candidate should also have spent some time researching the business as well as the vacant position. If possible, it is good to know a bit about the person who will be conducting the interview.

Acquiring information before an interview

Once an individual has scheduled an interview with a particular company, he or she should seek to find out as much about that company as possible. There are a number of ways to go about this research. First, the candidate can simply ask the company to send along any brochures or promotional literature that might be helpful. He might also try to contact other businesses that work with the company, to ask them their opinions. A very simple way to procure some information is to do an internet search of the company, or to search at the local library for articles about the business. Finally, a candidate can make use of his own business network, to try and discern the reputation of the business in the local community.

Objectives of a job interview

Too often, students assume that a job interview is always given with an eye towards getting a particular job. While this may be the usual case, it is also perfectly appropriate to interview so that one can discover more about the job, as well as about one's place in the job market. Many times, individuals will interview for a number of jobs they have no intention of taking, for the sole purpose of polishing their interview skills. It is important to determine the objectives of an interview beforehand. One danger that candidates run when they interview only to seek information, however, is that they will discover mid-interview that they would like the job and have not done adequate preparatory work for the interview. For this reason, it is always best to be prepared.

Listening skills in a job interview

One common misunderstanding of job interviews is that they are simply opportunities to deliver a rehearsed monologue of skills and achievements. In actuality, the ability to listen well may be more impressive to a potential employer. The candidate should make sure neither to interrupt the interviewer, nor to complete his or her sentences. When unsure about something the interviewer has said, it is always better to ask for clarification than to pretend comprehension. Too often, candidates are so focused on what they intend to say that they do not pay adequate attention to the tone and nuance of the interviewer; a well-prepared candidate should never have to worry about forgetting his or her lines.

Areas of inquiry for a job candidate

A candidate who doesn't have any questions about the employer during the interview is, whether intentionally or not, conveying the idea that he does not really care about the company. A candidate should always inquire about a few key areas. First, who are the business' chief competitors, and how does the business distinguish itself? What is the leadership structure of the business, and how long has the present leadership been in place?

What particular issues and problems is the business dealing with at present? Does the company have a particular set of values? What is the "culture" of the company? Have there been any major changes in the business or in the industry as a whole that will affect the business in the near future? Questions like these convey to a potential employer that the candidate has a real interest in the business.

Closed questions in a job interview

In a job interview, closed questions should be the easiest to answer, although they may not be the most pleasant. Closed questions are those that require just a one- or two-word answer. Such questions might include whether the candidate has a college degree, what their grade point average was, or whether they have ever done similar work. Usually, these questions are asked to verify the information listed in the individual's resume, or to introduce lines of conversation that will then be developed more fully. As a candidate, one should avoid elaborating too fully on these kinds of questions, particularly if such elaboration might be seen as making excuses or qualifying negative aspects of a resume. One should simply answer these questions and move on.

Open questions in a job interview

Open questions are those that require more than just a simple one-word answer. An open question might invite a candidate to describe a past work experience, or to detail what it is he finds interesting about the company. These are good questions for well-prepared candidates, because they give him a chance to accentuate positive aspects of his resume, as well as to avoid mentioning qualities that might be viewed less favorably. One of the common dangers of these questions, however, is that they may lead to vague responses. If the candidate feels unsure of exactly how to answer an open question, there is nothing wrong with politely asking the interviewer to narrow the question or break it down into some simpler parts.

Leading questions in a job interview

Leading questions are posed with an eye towards some further line of conversation. Leading questions can be very dangerous for a candidate if he is not well prepared. As an example, an interviewer might insinuate that one of the candidate's previous bosses was unfair or incompetent. While this may or may not be true, sometimes interviewers will use such a line of questioning to determine whether a job candidate is likely to be overly critical of authority, or to pass the buck. The best thing to do in an introductory interview is to remain diplomatic when presented with opportunities to be critical. A good candidate will not suggest that he is incapable of criticizing others, but will always emphasize his own responsibility as the most important concern.

Screening Interview Stage

The first in the series of job interviews is the screening interview. During screening interviews, a company is just trying to narrow down a large field of potential candidates. These interviews may not be performed by the same individuals that will conduct later interviews, and they may even be performed over the phone. For this reason, candidates should always be prepared for a screening interview. This means having a copy of one's resume and cover letter close to the phone, and being able to provide succinct answers to basic questions. The main point of a screening interview is to ensure that candidates have the basic qualifications and skills to be further considered for vacancies.

Selection and Confirmation Stage

After the initial screening interview, a candidate should assume that her basic skills and achievements are known by the company. So, in the next interview (known as a selection interview), the goal should be to make clear what other skills the candidate will be able to bring to the business. If the selection interview goes well, there will be a final interview, known as the confirmation interview. In some cases, the confirmation interview is a formality, in which the top executives get a chance to meet candidates who have already been approved for hire by the human resources department. Candidates who make it to a confirmation interview should just be polite, and not try too hard to sell themselves.

Job-Hunting

As part of preparing students for entry into the job market, teachers need to show them the various places to look for jobs. One of the best places to find a job is still the classified ad section of the local newspaper. However, there are now many on-line listings for jobs as well. These are constantly changing, so business teachers will want to keep abreast of the most popular sites. Many part-time and odd jobs will be advertised on bulletin boards and message boards at local supermarkets and libraries. Magazines and trade journals often have job listings, too. One of the most obvious yet often overlooked ways to get a job is simply to ask for one. If students are interested in working for a particular company, they should have the skills and wherewithal to call and inquire about openings.

Promoting Business Education Programs

Teachers should be familiar with some ways of promoting their classes to the local community, so that they can develop helpful relationships with local businesses. One good way to do this is by interacting with the community advisory councils from local businesses and municipal groups. These are committees whose only purpose is to discover ways in which the business can create positive connections with their community. Obviously, a great way for them to do this is by setting up relationships with local schools, and so they can become a wonderful resource for business teachers. Through partnerships with community advisory councils, business teachers can set up mentoring, job-shadowing, or internship programs, organize class trips, or simply acquire useful information about contemporary business practices.

Labor Force, Unemployment Rate, and Full Employment

The *labor force* is the total number of employed and unemployed individuals in a society. Unemployed individuals are those who are out of work but are actively seeking work. Individuals out of work and not seeking work are voluntarily unemployed and so are not considered part of the labor force.
The *unemployment rate* is the percentage of the labor force that is unemployed.
Full employment, surprisingly, does not mean that the unemployment rate is zero. Instead, what is called *full employment* is defined as an unemployment rate of six percent. This is because economists do not believe it is realistic to expect that the unemployment rate will ever drop below this level even under the best circumstances because of natural and seasonal causes of unemployment.

Seasonal Unemployment and Frictional Unemployment

Seasonal unemployment is the inevitable result of labor fluctuations during the course of a year. In agriculture, for example, employment increases a great deal during the peak harvest season and then decreases during the winter. In some cold climates, construction workers may be unemployed throughout the winter months.

Frictional unemployment is the result of the huge numbers of people entering and leaving the job market at any given time. There is always a lag time between deciding to look for a job and finding one, and individuals experiencing this lag time are considered frictionally unemployed. Every economy has a bit of frictional unemployment, although some say that the policy of unemployment compensation in the United States encourages more frictional unemployment than is necessary.

Structural Unemployment

Structural unemployment develops when changes in the industry result in a mismatch between the jobs available and the skills possessed by the workers. This has occurred in the United States' shoe industry: Workers no longer have the training to operate the requisite equipment but still demand a higher rate of pay, so the jobs have gone overseas. Structural unemployment can last much longer than other forms of unemployment as workers struggle to acquire new skills. Some people suggest that the government could remedy this problem by helping to pay for structurally unemployed citizens to get the training they need, or for workers to move to locations where they can be paid for the skills they already have.

Cyclical Unemployment

Cyclical unemployment is a lack of jobs resulting from the lack of demand in an economy. Essentially, cyclical unemployment is the unemployment left over after all the unemployment for structural, seasonal, and frictional reasons has been taken out. Because most economic models suggest that the usual combined rate of unemployment by for structural, seasonal, and frictional reasons is six percent, any increase greater than six percent is considered cyclical unemployment. The government tries to increase aggregate demand and minimize cyclical unemployment through macroeconomic policy; most of the unemployment data collected by the government is actually aimed at minimizing cyclical unemployment. Every economy, however, will experience decreases in demand from time to time.

Practice Test

Practice Questions

1. A command economy is characterized by:
    a. A *laissez-faire* approach by the government
    b. A moderate amount of government intervention in the economy
    c. Businesses commanding all aspects of the economy
    d. The government controlling prices and production

2. Which of the following is not a responsibility of the Securities and Exchange Commission (SEC)?
    a. Regulating securities
    b. Investigating insider trading
    c. Setting interest rates
    d. Processing applications for initial public offerings (IPOs)

3. In marketing, the demand for a product is directly influenced by:
    a. Customers' desire for a product
    b. Customers' ability to obtain a product
    c. Availability of a product
    d. Both A and B

4. The Sarbanes-Oxley Act of 2002:
    a. Vastly reduced the financial reporting obligations that corporations face
    b. Deregulated public utilities
    c. Was intended to fight corporate and accounting fraud
    d. Reduced tariffs on trade among North American countries

5. An employee earns $2,000.00 per month in gross pay, but pays $104.36 for health insurance, 9% in federal taxes, 3% for state taxes, and 2% for local taxes. What is the employee's net pay?
    a. $2,000.00
    b. $1,615.64
    c. $1,820.00
    d. $1,720.00

6. A market in which product availability exceeds demand is called a:
    a. Free market
    b. Seller's market
    c. Buyer's market
    d. Black market

7. Which of the following is not a part of Maslow's hierarchy of needs?
    a. Self-actualization
    b. Esteem
    c. Safety
    d. Supply and demand

8. Which of the following countries is not part of NAFTA?
    a. Mexico
    b. United States
    c. Canada
    d. China

9. A consumer's credit score is directly influenced by which of the following factors?
    a. Debt repayment history
    b. Employment history over the last five years
    c. Marital status
    d. Income level

10. Upon which organization does the international community primarily rely to deal with claims of unfair protectionism by one country against another?
    a. North Atlantic Treaty Organization (NATO)
    b. World Trade Organization (WTO)
    c. Organization of Petroleum Exporting Countries (OPEC)
    d. International Red Cross (IRC)

11. A homeowner is attempting to choose between several mortgage loans for a $200,000 home. Which of the following would have the lowest monthly payment?
    a. A 30-year fixed rate mortgage at 6%
    b. A 15-year fixed rate mortgage at 7%
    c. A 30-year fixed rate mortgage at 12%
    d. A 15-year fixed rate mortgage at 12%

12. The biggest factor that leads American companies to manufacture their products overseas in developing countries like China and India is:
    a. Higher quality of craftsmanship
    b. Lower labor costs
    c. Decreased transportation costs
    d. Effective legal systems

13. Which of the following correctly summarizes the accounting equation for a sole proprietorship?
    a. Assets = Liabilities + Owners' equity
    b. Liabilities = Assets + Owners' equity
    c. Owner's equity = Assets + Liabilities
    d. Revenue = Assets – Liabilities

14. In order to present a business plan to a group of potential investors, a businessperson would most likely use which software?
    a. Powerpoint
    b. Quickbooks
    c. Peoplesoft
    d. Excel

15. In order to start an online business, and individual would need all but which of the following:
    a. A business model
    b. A website
    c. An email address
    d. A fax machine

16. Which of the following types of assets would not be subject to depreciation?
    a. Heavy equipment
    b. Computers
    c. Real estate
    d. Company vehicles

17. When itemizing deductions on a federal tax return, an individual taxpayer may be able to deduct all but which of the following?
    a. Interest paid on a mortgage
    b. Charitable donations
    c. Losses from theft
    d. Groceries

18. Which of the following terms best describes a situation where an individual enters into an agreement with a company to use the company's business model within a given territory, usually in exchange for a fee?
    a. Sole proprietorship
    b. Limited liability corporation
    c. Franchise
    d. Incorporation

19. The par value of a bond is the:
    a. Average interest rate paid by a given type of bond over subsequent issues
    b. Amount of time until the bond matures
    c. Amount paid when the bond matures
    d. Amount of interest that the bond pays

20. Which of the following best describes Congress' purpose in setting up Freddie Mac in 1970?
    a. Expanding opportunities for home ownership
    b. Deregulating the credit market
    c. Improving regulation of the Internet
    d. Creating a place for small businesses to get loans

21. Which of the following countries would be considered an emerging market?
    a. Japan
    b. India
    c. Britain
    d. Canada

22. If the exchange rate between the Euro (€) and the U.S. dollar ($) is $2.5 to € 1, how many dollars would it take to purchase a plane ticket that costs € 1580.00?
    a. $39,500.00
    b. $3,950.00
    c. $395.00
    d. $632.00

23. If the U.S. Federal Reserve concludes that there is a significant risk of inflation, it will most likely:
    a. Raise interest rates
    b. Lower interest rates
    c. Keep interest rates the same
    d. Decrease bond yields

24. A combination of slow economic growth and high inflation is called:
    a. Inflationary pressure
    b. Deflation
    c. Stagflation
    d. Disinflation

25. A shareholder owns 200 shares of stock XYZ at $58 each. If there is a 2-1 stock split, how many shares will that shareholder have, and what will the new share price be?
    a. 100 shares at $116 per share
    b. 200 shares at $116 per share
    c. 400 shares at $29 per share
    d. 400 shares at $58 per share

26. Which of the following is not true of stock dividends?
    a. They are usually taxable
    b. They are offered voluntarily by companies in order to make their stock more attractive
    c. Their amount and frequency are determined directly by shareholders at large
    d. They may be discontinued or reduced at any time

27. If a stock has a high P/E ratio, this means that:
    a. The stock's price is low considering the value of the company's earnings
    b. The stock pays a high dividend based on its earnings per share
    c. The stock's price is high considering the value of its earnings per share
    d. The company's earnings per share are high

28. An individual who is about to retire and wants to earn interest without risking his or her principal would most likely be advised to invest in:
    a. Value stocks
    b. An index fund
    c. A mutual fund
    d. U.S. Treasury bonds

29. A company that is included in the Dow Jones Industrial Average most likely to be:
    a. A well-known corporation with a large market capitalization
    b. A foreign company
    c. A start-up that was recently listed on the stock exchange
    d. A small- to mid-sized technology company

Table 1

	Investor A	**Investor B**	**Investor C**	**Investor D**
Stocks	20%	85%	70%	50%
Bonds	70%	10%	20%	50%
Cash	10%	5%	10%	0%

30. Which of the investors in Table 1 has the portfolio that is exposed to the greatest amount of risk?
    a. Investor A
    b. Investor B
    c. Investor C
    d. Investor D

31. Refer again to Table 1. If Investor D's stocks have an average return of 8.8% during the year, and Investor D's bonds have an average return of 5.2%, what is the average overall return on Investor D's portfolio?
    a. 14%
    b. 7%
    c. 5.6%
    d. Cannot be determined

32. If one is planning to start a small business, which should one do first?
    a. Obtain a business loan
    b. Find a partner
    c. Assess one's personal financial situation
    d. Choose a location for one's business

33. Frank is 33 years old and married, with 2 children. He has $40,000 in his retirement account, which is earning an average of 5% annually, and $10,000 in his personal savings account, which is earning 2% annually. He is current with his mortgage, and has $50,000 left to pay at a rate of 6%. Frank also has $30,000 in credit card debt with an average rate of 13%. If Frank wants to increase his chances of retiring comfortably, what would the best way be for him to spend a Christmas bonus of $10,000?
    a. Put it in his retirement account
    b. Put it in his savings account
    c. Use half to pay down his mortgage and save the other half
    d. Use all of it to pay down his credit card debt

34. If a country is a net exporter, this means that:
    a. The value of the goods that it imports exceeds the value of the goods that it exports
    b. The value of the goods that it exports exceeds the value of the goods that it imports
    c. It exports consumer products
    d. It has high tariffs

35. If a government implements an import tariff on consumer electronics, what is it most likely trying to accomplish?
    a. It is trying to protect its domestic consumer electronics industry from competition
    b. It is trying to decrease the cost of imported consumer electronics
    c. It is trying to discourage domestic companies from producing consumer electronics
    d. It is trying to increase competition and lower prices in the consumer electronics industry

36. If a potential business owner projects that she will need to invest $100,000 in equipment to start a dry cleaning business, and the business' monthly expenses on rent, insurance, labor costs, and other incidentals is $5,000, how many months will it take for her to earn back her initial investment if the average monthly gross revenue is $8,000?
    a. Less than 9 months
    b. Less than 20 months
    c. Less than 34 months
    d. None of the above

Table 2

	Sticker price of the car	Down payment	Monthly payment	Term of loan	
Option A	$8,000	$0	$330	36 months	11880
Option B	$8,000	$3,000	$160	60 months	12600
Option C	$15,000	$0	$250	60 months	15000
Option D	$15,000	$5,000	$400	36 months	19400

37. Refer to Table 2 above. A family wants to buy a new car, and is trying to decide between four different car and car loan options. Which of the loans would require them to pay the least amount of money overall, including the down payment and the monthly payments?
    a. Option A
    b. Option B
    c. Option C
    d. Option D

38. Which of the four options listed in Table 2 would require the family to pay the least amount of interest, total?
    a. Option A
    b. Option B
    c. Option C
    d. Option D

39. Which of the options listed in Table 2 would require the family to pay the highest amount of interest, total?
    a. Option A
    b. Option B
    c. Option C
    d. Option D

Use Table 3 to answer Questions 40 and 41:

Table 3	Cost	Franchise fee	Average gross monthly revenue	Average monthly expenses
Business A	$500,000	5% of gross revenue	$20,000	$15,000
Business B	$440,000	4% of gross revenue	$16,000	$10,000
Business C	$320,000	None	$10,000	$5,000
Business D	$175,000	None	$8,000	$5,000

40. Refer to Table 3. Sarah has up to $550,000 to invest, and is trying to decide which of four catering businesses she wants to purchase. Which of the options below correctly lists the businesses in order of average monthly profit from largest to smallest when the franchise fee is taken into consideration?
    a. A, B, C, D
    b. C, D, A, B
    c. B, C, A, D
    d. C, B, A, D

41. If Sarah wanted to get her initial investment back as quickly as possible, which of the following options would you advise her to choose, based upon Table 3 information?
    a. Business A
    b. Business B
    c. Business C
    d. Business D

42. A consumer's credit score may be factor in all but which of the following transactions?
    a. Buying a car
    b. Buying a home
    c. Getting a personal loan
    d. Opening a bank account

43. Comprehensive car insurance typically covers:
    a. Damage the insured does to the property of others while driving the insured vehicle
    b. Medical expenses others incur as a result of a collision with the insured vehicle
    c. Damage done to the insured's vehicle by someone else
    d. All of the above

44. Which of the following is not typically cited as a potential cause of oil price increases?
    a. Price increases for consumer goods and services in the U.S.
    b. Increased global demand for oil
    c. Speculation in the oil market
    d. Insufficient refinery capacity

45. Nations whose economies rely primarily of the export of non-oil commodities like rubber or copper are:
    a. Typically located in Northern and Western Europe
    b. Often referred to as "developing countries" or "emerging markets"
    c. Known for their world class education systems
    d. Among usually among the wealthiest countries in the world

46. A company considering manufacturing a product in several different emerging markets will most likely consider which of the following factors in choosing between them?
    a. Likelihood of political instability
    b. Labor costs and regulations
    c. Cost of shipping goods from that country to the destination country
    d. All of the above

47. Adam Smith is best known for:
    a. Founding the doctrine of mercantilism
    b. Supporting the spread of communism
    c. Arguing for free market economics
    d. Arguing that the government should redistribute income

48. According to standard economic theories, countries that have a comparative advantage in the production of cotton should:
    a. Export another product, and import cotton
    b. Export cotton, and import other products
    c. Implement tariffs to protect their domestic cotton industry
    d. Work hard to reduce their comparative advantage and diversify their economy

49. An advantage of protectionism for countries that implement it is that it:
    a. Improves the country's global competitiveness
    b. Ensures that domestic jobs will be retained in the short term
    c. Encourages economic growth
    d. Prevents corruption

50. GDP measures a country's:
    a. Employment level
    b. Education level
    c. Total economic output
    d. Wage levels

51. A human resources manager is likely to be responsible for all but which of the following:
    a. Sales
    b. Payroll
    c. Hiring
    d. Training

52. The main function of a human resources department is to:
   a. Meet the company's recruiting goals
   b. Maximize employee productivity while minimizing pay
   c. Facilitate communication between the employer and the employees
   d. Prevent lawsuits

53. Which of the following questions would it be illegal to ask a job candidate at a pre-employment interview?
   a. Have you ever requested workers' compensation benefits?
   b. Do you have any disabilities that would interfere with your ability to perform this job?
   c. Both A and B
   d. Neither A nor B

54. Technological aids can be used to directly fulfill all but which of the following human resources functions:
   a. Soliciting resumes for open positions
   b. Assessing a new employee's job readiness
   c. Communicating information about employee benefits
   d. Resolving disputes between employees and management

55. A new manager with ABC Industries has noticed that many of his employees are chronically late to work. To remedy the problem, the manager decides to implement a bonus system that will financially reward employees who are on time to work for ten consecutive days. According to B.F. Skinner's Operant Conditioning theory, what type of behavior modification approach is the manager using?
   a. Extinction
   b. Punishment
   c. Negative reinforcement
   d. Positive reinforcement

Use Table 4 to answer Question 56:

Management Approach	Characteristic
1. Classical Theory	A. Productivity can be improved through the application of mathematical models
2. Behavioral Theory	B. Understanding the worker's perspective is key to successful management
3. Management Science Approach	C. There is no single "correct" theory; instead, managers should apply the theory that is most sensible in a given situation
4. Contingency Approach	D. Productivity can be maximized by presenting the right combination of incentives, and correctly designing jobs

56. Refer to Table 4, and correctly match each Management Approach in the right column with the characteristic in the left column that best describes it.
    a. 1-D, 2-B, 3-A, 4-C
    b. 1-A, 2-C, 3-B, 4-D
    c. 1-A, 2-C, 3-D, 4-B
    d. 1-D, 2-A, 3-B, 4-C

57. A successful manager will be able to effectively delegate:
    a. Responsibility
    b. Accountability
    c. Authority
    d. Ability

58. According to Fayol's Administrative Theory of Management, which of the following is a correct list of the five essential functions of management?
    a. Controlling, composing, planning, organizing, implementing
    b. Containing, controlling, implementing, planning, organizing
    c. Composing, coordinating, controlling, planning, organizing
    d. Controlling, commanding, coordinating, planning, organizing

59. According to the National Environmental Policy Act of 1967, a business is required to prepare an environmental impact statement (EIS) when it:
    a. Hires a new worker
    b. Makes a charitable contribution
    c. Develops a new marketing initiative
    d. Builds a new factory

60. A manufacturing company implements anti-pollution measures as outlined by applicable legislation, but opts not to adopt any additional anti-pollution measures. This company has most likely adopted which of the following approaches to business-society relations?
    a. Social Responsiveness Approach
    b. Social Responsibility Approach
    c. Social Obligation Approach
    d. Cost-benefit Approach

61. Which of the following constitutes a binding contract?
    a. An agreement signed and dated by one party and one witness
    b. An agreement signed and dated by both parties
    c. An agreement signed by both parties and witnessed by a third party
    d. An agreement signed and dated by both parties and a witness

62, Corporation X, the largest oil refiner in the U.S., wants to purchase Corporation Y, the only other oil refiner in the U.S. This situation may be of concern to the government because:
    a. It may violate environmental laws
    b. It may constitute a violation of antitrust laws
    c. It could violate labor laws by reducing employees' choice of employers
    d. It could constitute a pyramid scheme

63. The Equal Employment Opportunity Commission (EEOC) is responsible for enforcing all but which of the following laws?
    a. Civil Rights Act of 1964
    b. Equal Pay Act
    c. Environmental Protection Act
    d. Americans with Disabilities Act

64. Anna is interested in purchasing a computer for her small landscaping business. She wants to be able to compose simple fliers and advertising materials, communicate with clients via email, and order supplies online. Which of the following lists best describes the hardware and software components that Anna's computer should have?
    a. Internet connection, Quickbooks, and at least 10 GB of memory
    b. Word processing software, Quickbooks, and an Internet connection
    c. Word processing software, an Internet connection, and 1-5 GB of memory
    d. Quickbooks, an Internet connection, and 1-5 GB of memory

65. Microsoft Excel would most likely be used for which of the following tasks?
    a. Developing a strategic plan
    b. Filing invoices
    c. Creating a sales presentation
    d. Analyzing numerical sales data

66. Which of the following steps might a company take in order to prevent unauthorized individuals from accessing confidential data?
    a. Requiring a username and password to access its computer system
    b. Constructing a firewall to protect its computer system
    c. Both A and B
    d. Neither A nor B

67. In order to facilitate communication between employees within a company, the company is considering providing all employees with unlimited access to a file that contains employee names, work phone numbers and addresses, work email addresses, birthdates, and social security numbers. What confidentiality issues would this new policy raise?
    a. None, the value of improved communication between employees would outweigh any confidentiality issues
    b. Many employees may object to their social security numbers and birthdays being shared with others; the company should publish the birthdays anyway, but withhold the social security numbers
    c. Many employees may object to their social security numbers and birthdays being shared with others; the company should withhold both of these
    d. Releasing of any of this information is a violation of employees' privacy

68. A business education teacher has allotted one class period to help students identify potential career options. Which of the following activities would be most appropriate given these circumstances?
    a. Having students complete an internship
    b. Having each student deliver a five-minute presentation describing their parents' jobs
    c. Administering a test that advises students about what careers might fit their interests and talents
    d. Asking students to write an essay describing their "dream job"

69. Which of the following business careers could a teacher safely recommend for a student who would not enjoy working with the public on a regular basis?
    a. Financial advisor
    b. Insurance salesperson
    c. Real estate agent
    d. None of the above

70. Choose the list below that best describes the most important contents of a resume:
    a. Salary requirements, relevant work experience, educational attainment, objective
    b. Contact information, grade point average, relevant work experience, objective
    c. References, objective, educational attainment, salary requirements
    d. Contact information, objective, educational attainment, relevant work experience

71. At a meeting with shareholders, an executive would be most likely to use which of the following visual aids to present a report on monthly stock gains and losses over a one-year period?
    a. Bar chart
    b. Pie chart
    c. Line graph
    d. Scatterplot

72. When manually proofreading a business document for a colleague, which of the following answers describes the correct way one would indicate that a section of text should be removed?
    a. An X should be drawn through the text
    b. A caret should be drawn at the beginning and end of the text
    c. A diagonal line should be drawn through the text from bottom left to top right
    d. A horizontal line should be drawn through the text with a loop at the right end of the line

73. When researching a presentation about a national shipping business, the most detailed and comprehensive source of information about the top management of the company and its competitors would most likely be:
    a. Microfilm records from local newspapers
    b. Hoovers.com
    c. LexisNexis.com
    d. The catalogue at your local library

74. Which of the following lists contains only types of computer software?
    a. Internet, Microsoft Office, Quicken
    b. Motherboard, Quicken, Excel
    c. Quicken, Peoplesoft, Microsoft Office
    d. Monitor, Mouse, Keyboard

75. Search engine optimization (SEO) is the process of:
    a. Designing a search engine to operate as efficiently as possible
    b. Designing a website to maximize its placement in search engine results for particular keywords, thus increasing traffic to the site
    c. Improving the visual aesthetic of a search engine
    d. Making a search engine more user-friendly

76. On the Internet, links are used in all but which of the following ways?
    a. They direct Internet users to other websites that have additional relevant information
    b. They are used for marketing purposes, to entice Internet users to navigate away from one website to view another one
    c. They allow Internet users to open additional windows that explain a webpage's content or provide technical assistance
    d. They allow computer users to open software programs on their PC

77. When designing a website for an online business, the web developer would include a site map in order to:
    a. Give website users directions to the business
    b. Provide website users with a list of links to all of the pages on the website
    c. Convince website users that it is safe to purchase products from the website
    d. Help website users decide which products to buy from the website

78. Better Business Bureau certification is useful for businesses that engage in e-commerce because it:
    a. Protects them from legal action by defrauded consumers
    b. Exempts them from paying state taxes
    c. Proves that they are certified by the government
    d. Reassures customers that the company is reliable

79. Businesses can increase the security of confidential customer information by:
    a. Destroying paper records of credit card information
    b. Conducting employee background checks
    c. Installing a firewall and virus protection software for computer systems
    d. All of the above

80. A high school student expresses interest in starting her own auto repair business after graduating from high school. She could best prepare for such a career by:
    a. Getting a college degree in finance and then completing an MBA program
    b. Taking small business finance, law, and accounting courses
    c. Getting an internship or part time job at an auto-repair shop
    d. B and C only

81. A business education teacher wants to evaluate her program in terms of how well graduates are prepared for the workforce. Which of the following strategies would be most likely to provide the best data to answer this question?

    a. Setting up an advisory committee of local employers to gather feedback on graduates' performance in the workplace

    b. Asking students to complete internships with local employers

    c. Conducting a survey of recent graduates to see if they were able to find jobs with local employers

    d. Asking the business professors at a local community college to provide feedback

82. Which of the following activities that are conducted by high school student leadership organizations would be the most effective tool for teaching business skills?

    a. Raising money by selling concessions at athletic events

    b. Performing community service by painting a local elementary school

    c. Holding an awards ceremony to honor scholarship winners

    d. Tutoring middle school students in math and reading

83. A business education teacher is asked to serve as an advisor to the local chapter of a student leadership organization. The teacher's primary responsibility as an advisor is most likely to:

    a. Ensure that students follow established procedures for conducting meetings

    b. Ensure the health and safety of student participants in the organization

    c. Design and implement activities for the group

    d. Collect and account for dues and fundraising proceeds

84. Which of the following activities provides the best example of collaboration between business education teachers and teachers of other subject areas?

    a. Students in a business education class are asked to write cover letters and resumes

    b. Students in a business education class read case studies about research and development for new products

    c. A business education teacher and a math teacher coordinate their lesson plans so that the concepts taught in math class are subsequently applied to real situations in the business class

    d. Students in a business class learn to balance checkbooks

85. Which of the following activities would most effectively and comprehensively assess students' mastery of learning objectives for a unit about small business?

    a. Asking students to create and market a new invention

    b. Asking students to design and implement a community service project

    c. Requiring students to complete an internship or externship

    d. Having students write and present a business plan

86. A business education teacher wants students to complete an activity that teaches them skills that are necessary for working in a culturally diverse environment. Which of the following activities would fulfill this goal?

    a. Collaborating with the social studies teacher to teach students about work customs in other cultures

    b. Asking students to read and discuss written accounts of minorities' experiences in the workplace

    c. Teaching students about laws and regulations that protect people from diverse ethnic and cultural backgrounds

    d. All of the above

Use Table 5 to answer Question 87:

Name of Business	Credit Rating
Business A	BBB
Business B	BB
Business C	AA
Business D	AAA

87. Based on the information in Table 5, which of the following lists correctly orders the businesses from least to most risky for investors?

    a. Business B, Business A, Business C, Business D

    b. Business A, Business B, Business D, Business C

    c. Business D, Business C, Business A, Business B

    d. Business C, Business D, Business B, Business A

Use Table 6 to answer Questions 88 and 89:

Time card: Scott Smith		
Date	Clock in	Clock out
11/01	11:00 AM	3:00 PM
11/02	8:00 AM	12:00 PM
11/03	8:00 AM	12:00 PM
11/05	11:00 AM	3:00 PM
11/07	8:00 AM	12:00 PM

88. If part time employee Scott Smith, whose time card is shown in Table 6, is paid $10.00 per hour on weekdays (Monday-Friday), and $11.00 per hour on weekends, and November 1st is a Monday, how much should he be paid for the week of November 1st through November 7th?

    a. $160.00

    b. $200.00

    c. $204.00

    d. $240.00

89. Only full time employees of Scott Smith's company, whose time card is shown in Table 6, have health insurance and 401k benefits deducted from their paychecks. Based on the number of hours Smith worked from November 1st through November 7th, which of the following is a correct list of his payroll deductions if he is a W-4 employee?
    a. 401k and health insurance
    b. Social security and Medicare
    c. Social security, Medicare, and income taxes
    d. None of the above

90. The company that Scott Smith works for provides full time employees with a 100% 401k match after one year on the job if they contribute 4% of their paycheck. If Scott becomes a full time employee after a year, makes $2,000 per paycheck, and contributes 4% to his 401k each pay period, how much would the company have to contribute to his 401k during each pay period?
    a. $160
    b. $80
    c. $40
    d. Cannot be determined

[handwritten: 4% = .04   40% = .4]

91. Accounts receivable are:
    a. Fixed assets
    b. Fixed liabilities
    c. Current assets
    d. Current liabilities

92. Owners' equity is comprised of:
    a. The personal net worth of the owners plus the amount of their initial investment in the business
    b. The amount of the owners' initial investment in the business
    c. The owners' unclaimed profits from the business' operation
    d. Both B and C

93. Which of the following are not protected by copyright law?
    a. Architectural drawings
    b. Scripts for plays
    c. Advertising slogans
    d. Books of poetry

94. A phrase that is associated with a particular product would be protected by which of the following?
    a. Trademark law
    b. Patent law
    c. Copyright law
    d. Both A and C

95. Which of the following is true of a corporation?
    a. It is always owned by shareholders
    b. Its shareholders are personally liable if it fails
    c. Its board of directors is personally liable if it fails
    d. It cannot sue another entity or be sued

96. Which of the following would be a violation of the Occupational Safety and Health Act (OSHA)?
    a. An employee becoming injured while commuting to work
    b. An employee becoming injured because an employer did not provide equipment in good working order
    c. An employer requiring employees to work with toxic chemicals
    d. An employer failing to accompany an OSHA compliance officer on an inspection

97. The following are each sentences from a job description. Select the sentence that clearly and correctly communicates its intended meaning.
    a. The employee, will have excellent oral communication skills.
    b. The employees oral communication skills will be excellent.
    c. The employee will communicate orally and in writing well.
    d. The employee will have excellent writing skills.

98. Which of the following is true of a Wide Area Network (WAN)?
    a. A WAN is equivalent to a LAN
    b. Businesses usually have their own WAN
    c. The Internet is an example of a WAN
    d. Businesses prefer WANs to LANs because their data transfer speed is higher

99. A business education teacher teaches two classes of 30 9th graders during a semester. At the end of the class, students are given identical tests of the course material. Students in Class 1, which was taught using a traditional lecture approach, scored an average of 73% on the test. Students in Class 2, which was taught using interactive exercises and computer-based simulations, scored an average of 82% on the test. What can be concluded from this experiment?
    a. The students in Class 2 are more intelligent than those in Class 1
    b. The teaching methods used for Class 2 are superior to those used for Class 1
    c. Nothing can be concluded from these results because one semester is not a long enough period of time to accurately measure learning
    d. Nothing can be concluded from these results because students' baseline performance on these tests was not measured before the experiment

100. Which of the following would violate federal child labor regulations?
    a. Hiring your own child to work in your small business if the child is under 14
    b. Employing someone under 14 as a newspaper carrier
    c. Employing someone under 18 in a job deemed hazardous
    d. Employing anyone under 18 as a babysitter

Answers and Explanations

1. D: A command economy (also known as a planned economy) is characterized by the government controlling nearly all aspects of the economy, including prices and production. This type of economy is traditionally associated with Communist economies where prices, wages and production quotas are set by the government. A, B, and C are all incorrect because they imply some form of private sector autonomy.

2. C: The Securities and Exchange Commission (SEC) is responsible for regulating securities, investigating insider trading, and processing applications for initial public offerings (IPOs) of stock. However, the Federal Reserve is responsible for setting interest rates.

3. D: In marketing, the demand for a product is determined both by customers' desire for that product, coupled with their ability to obtain it if they want it. For example, even if customers want a product, demand for it may be decreased if it is illegal or prohibitively expensive. Answer C, availability of a given product, refers to supply, not demand.

4. C: The Sarbanes-Oxley Act of 2002 was intended to fight corporate and accounting fraud in the wake of several huge scandals that brought down major U.S corporations. This bill reformed the rules and regulations governing corporations' financial disclosures, and increased financial reporting obligations.

5. B: The employee's net pay, or total take-home pay after deductions, is $1,615.64. This is calculated by subtracting the employee's taxes (totaling 14%, or $280.00) and insurance ($104.36) from the gross pay of $2,000.00.

6. C: A market in which product availability is greater than product demand is called a buyer's market, because when supply (product availability) exceeds demand, the prices paid by buyers decrease. This decrease in prices benefits the buyer of a product and decreases the seller's profits.

7. D: Supply and demand is not a part of Maslow's hierarchy of needs. This hierarchy is part of Maslow's theory that once people satisfy basic needs like food, water, and physical security, they begin to pursue needs higher up the hierarchy, like social acceptance, self-esteem, and self-actualization.

8. D: China is not part of NAFTA. NAFTA refers to the North American Free Trade Agreement, which is an agreement to encourage trade between the U.S., Canada, and Mexico.

9. A: A consumer's credit score is directly influenced by the individual's payment history on car and home loans, credit cards, etc. While marital status, employment history, and income level may indirectly influence the credit score by affecting the consumer's ability to pay bills on time, only payment history itself is a direct factor in credit score calculations.

10. B: The primary organization upon which the international community relies to deal with claims of unfair protectionism by one country against another is the World Trade Organization (WTO). NATO is a military alliance among many North American and

European countries, OPEC is an organization of oil-producing countries that regulates supply and prices, and the Red Cross is an international humanitarian organization.

11. A: A 30-year fixed rate mortgage at 6% would provide the lowest monthly payment on the $200,000 mortgage loan, because it has both the longest term (30 years) and the lowest interest rate (6%). This means that the consumer would be paying less interest on a yearly basis, and the total would be divided over the maximum number of monthly payments.

12. B: The biggest factor that leads American companies to manufacture their products in developing countries is lower labor cost. Labor costs in developing countries (countries with a comparatively low GDP per capita) are lower than in the U.S. because unemployment is higher and labor regulations are less stringent.

13. A: The accounting equation for a sole proprietorship is correctly stated as Assets = Liabilities + Owners' equity. In the accounting equation for a corporation, owners' equity is replaced by shareholders' equity.

14. A: In order to present a business plan to a group of potential investors, a businessperson would most likely use Powerpoint, which allows an individual to present text and pictures in a slide format using a PC. Quickbooks is used for accounting, Peoplesoft is used by human resources professionals, and Excel is used for storing and analyzing numerical and categorical data.

15. D: In order to start an online business, an individual would need an Internet connection, email, and a web domain, but a fax machine would not necessarily be required, since documents can be scanned and sent via email.

16. C: Real estate is not subject to depreciation. While real estate often appreciates (increases) in value, assets like vehicles and computer equipment inevitably depreciate (decline in value) due to normal wear and tear.

17. D: When itemizing deductions on a federal tax return, a taxpayer may be able to deduct all of the things listed here except for food costs. Mortgage interest, losses from theft and charitable donations are all tax-deductible under certain circumstances.

18. C: When an individual enters into an agreement with a company to use the company's business model within a given territory, this is called a franchise agreement. In most cases, the individual pays the company a franchise fee, usually a percentage of gross revenue, in order to use the company's business model.

19. C: The par value of a bond is the value of the bond when it is issued. The par value is typically the amount that the bond issuer pays the buyer when the bond matures, as well.

20. A: Expanding opportunities for home ownership was Congress' primary purpose in setting up Freddie Mac. This organization was charged with increasing the availability of money for home loans by pooling mortgages together to create mortgage-backed securities.

21. B: India is the only country listed here that would be considered an emerging market. Emerging markets exist only in countries that are in the process of rapidly industrializing. Countries like Britain, Japan, and Canada have slower-growing, mature economies that have

long passed the emergent stage. As in the case of India, emerging markets are often the destination for outsourced jobs.

22. B: If the exchange rate between the Euro (€) and the U.S. dollar ($) is $2.5 to € 1, it would take $3,950.00 to purchase a plane ticket that costs € 1580.00. This is calculated by multiplying the number of dollars to one Euro (2.5) by the cost of the plane ticket in Euros (1580).

23. A: If the U.S. Federal Reserve concludes that there is a significant risk of inflation, it will most likely raise interest rates. By raising interest rates, a central bank like the Federal Reserve can increase the cost of borrowing money, thus slowing economic growth and the price inflation that results from increased demand.

24. C: A combination of slow economic growth and high inflation is called stagflation. This can occur when slow economic growth (little or none of the wage and job increases that create demand) is coupled with price increases caused by external factors like rising energy costs.

25. C: If a shareholder owns 200 shares of stock XYZ at $58 each and there is a 2-1 stock split, the shareholder would then own 400 shares at $29 per share. Companies split stock in order to decrease the price and stimulate trading. In a two for one split, the number of shares is doubled, but the price is halved.

26. C: Stock dividends are usually taxable, they may be discontinued or reduced at any time, and they are offered voluntarily by companies to make their stock more attractive. However, the amount and frequency of dividend payments are determined by the company's board of directors, not by shareholders at large.

27. C: If a stock has a high P/E ratio, this means that the stock's price is high considering the value of its earnings per share (EPS). The P/E ratio is calculated by dividing the share price by the company's EPS. The closer the result is to zero, the cheaper the stock is in relation to the amount of money the company is earning.

28. D: An individual who is about to retire and wants to earn interest without risking his or her principal would most likely be advised to invest in U.S. Treasury bonds. Value stocks, index funds, and mutual funds are all tied to the stock market, which is far more volatile and risky than U.S. Treasury bonds. (Some other bond investments, like junk bonds, can be quite risky). Since this investor is more concerned with protecting the principal than with earning high returns, an investment in bonds would best match his or her objective.

29. A: A company that is included in the Dow Jones Industrial Average most likely would be a well-known corporation with a large market capitalization. The Dow lists only thirty companies, most of which are household names.

30. B: Investor B is exposed to the greatest amount of risk, because 85% of the money in Investor B's portfolio is invested in stocks. Stocks are historically riskier than bonds or cash, so Investor B is more vulnerable than the other investors to large market fluctuations. However, this also means that Investor B has the largest potential to earn higher returns.

31. The correct answer is B, 7%. If stocks return 8.8% during the year, and bonds return 5.2%, then Investor D's overall return would be the average of both halves of the portfolio, since 50% was in bonds and 50% was in stocks. The overall return is equal to the weighted average of the returns from all investments, in this case the average of 8.8% and 5.2%.

32. C: If one is planning to start a small business, one's first step should be to assess one's personal financial situation in order to determine how much start-up capital one has, and how long one can afford to support oneself before one's business begins to turn a profit. Conducting these types of calculations will help one determine how large a loan one needs to request, and whether one needs a partner. Banks would also require this information before they issued a loan.

33. D: Frank could improve his chances for a comfortable retirement by using the $10,000 bonus to pay down his high interest credit card debt. Since the high interest rate on the credit card debt means that Frank is paying more in interest than he would be earning in either his savings account or his retirement account, paying down this debt will increase his ability to save over the long term. Since the credit card interest rate is higher than the mortgage interest rate, the credit card should be paid off first.

34. B: If a country is a net exporter, this means that the value of the goods that it exports exceeds the value of the goods that it imports. Net exporters have positive trade balances, meaning that the value of the goods that they sell to other countries exceeds the value of the goods that they buy from other countries.

35. A: If a government implements a tariff on imported consumer electronics, it is most likely trying to protect its domestic consumer electronics industry from foreign competition. By increasing tariffs, the government will increase the domestic prices for foreign-made consumer electronics, thus making domestically-produced products more attractive to consumers and reducing the overall level of competition in the industry.

36. C: If the business owner has invested $100,000 into the business, and makes an average monthly profit of $3,000 ($8,000 average gross revenue minus the $5,000 monthly costs of running the business), it will take approximately 33.3 months for her to make back her initial $100,000 investment.

37. A: If the family is looking for the lowest overall cost, Option A would total only $11,880 ($330 multiplied by 36 months). Option B would cost $12,600 overall, option C would cost $15,000, and option D would cost $19,400, including the down payment and monthly payments.

38. C: If the family wanted to ensure that they pay the lowest amount of interest possible, Option C would be the best choice. The total cost of the car, $15,000, divided by the number of payments (60) equals the monthly payment exactly, meaning that the family pays no interest at all for this option. Interest can be calculated by subtracting the car's sticker price from the total amount actually paid over the life of the loan.

39. B: Option B would require the family to pay the highest amount of interest total. Option B pays a total of $12,600 ($160 multiplied by 60 months plus $3000 in down payment) for an $8,000 vehicle, so $4,600 of that payment is interest. The others have lower interest payments.

40. C: Business B has the highest average monthly profit, at $5,360. This is calculated by adding the franchise fee to the total monthly expenditures, and subtracting this total from the average gross monthly revenue. Business C makes an average monthly profit of $5,000, Business A makes around $4,000 per month, and Business D makes just $3,000 per month.

41. D: If Sarah wanted to get her initial investment back as quickly as possible, she would be best advised to choose Business D, which would allow her to recoup her initial investment of $175,000 in just over 58 weeks. One can estimate how long it will take to recoup the initial investment for a business by dividing the cost of buying the business by the average monthly profit.

42. D: A consumer's credit score may be considered when a consumer buys a car or home if the transaction involves a loan, and it will also be considered if an individual applies for a personal loan. However, one's credit score is not considered when opening a bank account, because the account holder is depositing money rather than borrowing it.

43. D: Comprehensive insurance typically covers damage that the insured does to others and their property while driving the car, as well as damage that is done to the insured and the insured's property, assuming the other party is not insured. Collision insurance only covers damage done by the insured to others and their property.

44. A: Many economists argue that price increases for consumer goods and services in the U.S. increase as a result of oil price increases, but they are not typically cited as a potential cause of them.

45. B: Nations whose economies rely primarily on the export of non-oil commodities like rubber or copper are often referred to as "developing countries" or "emerging markets." Because of the instability of commodity prices, and these countries' often disproportionate reliance on commodity exports, developing countries are typically poorer and less able to provide social services than are countries that rely more heavily on manufacturing and service industries.

46. D: All of the above. Political instability could put the company's investment at risk, and the labor and shipping costs associated with a given country can be a decisive factor in investment decisions.

47. C: Adam Smith is best known for writing *The Wealth of Nations*, a treatise on free market economics in which he describes an "invisible hand" which guides the marketplace through individuals protecting their own self-interest. He argued that economic competition through a free market would be the best way to increase economic efficiency, productivity, and ultimately human happiness.

48. B: Economic theory states that countries with a comparative advantage in producing a particular product should produce and export that product, and use the proceeds to import the other products that they need from other countries.

49. B: An advantage of protectionism for countries that implement it is that it helps ensure that domestic jobs will be retained in the short term. By implementing protectionist measures that decrease the competitiveness of otherwise cheaper foreign goods,

governments can protect the domestic industries that produce those goods and preserve the jobs of the people who work in them.

50. C: GDP (gross domestic product) measures a country's total economic output, including goods and services, over a given period of time. Usually, GDP is reported annually.

51. A: A human resources manager is likely to be responsible for hiring, training, and payroll, but not sales. Human resources managers are in charge of employer-employee relations, including any activity that involves recruiting and retaining valuable employees.

52. C: The main function of a human resources department is to facilitate communication between the employer and the employees. While human resources departments are primarily responsible to the company's upper management, they are intended to provide a "neutral" conduit through which personnel policies can be devised and implemented, and through which employees can express and resolve concerns.

53. C: It would be illegal to ask either of the questions listed in answers A and B at a job interview. The Americans with Disabilities Act prohibits employers from attempting to ascertain a prospective employee's disability status prior to hiring the job candidate. Questions like, "Have you ever requested workers' compensation benefits," or, "Do you have any disabilities that would interfere with your ability to perform this job," would both fall into this category of illegal interview questions.

54. D: Technological aids such as email and computer software programs can be used to directly fulfill human resources functions like soliciting resumes for open positions, assessing a new employee's job readiness, or communicating information about employee benefits. However, a complicated situation such as an employee-employer dispute requires listening and negotiation skills and judgment that cannot be replaced by a computer.

55. D: The manager is using positive reinforcement. According to Skinner's theory, undesirable behavior such as tardiness can be dealt with using positive reinforcement, negative reinforcement, punishment, or extinction (discontinuing an existing practice that encourages or rewards that behavior).

56. A: The Classical Theory of management argues that productivity can be maximized by presenting the right combination of incentives, and correctly designing jobs. The Behavioral Theory emphasizes that understanding the worker's perspective is key to successful management, and the Management Science approach asserts that productivity can be improved through the application of mathematical models. More recently, proponents of the Contingency Approach have argued that there is no single "correct" theory; instead, managers should apply the theory that is most sensible in a given situation.

57. C: A successful manager will be able to effectively delegate authority. As a leader, the manager always retains accountability for results and ultimate responsibility for employees' actions. However, the manager must be able to delegate decision-making authority to subordinate employees in order to fulfill his or her job function. Ability D can be improved through training, but it cannot be automatically delegated.

58. D: According to Fayol's Administrative Theory of Management, the five essential functions of management are controlling, commanding, coordinating, planning, and

organizing. Henri Fayol, a French engineer, pioneered the Classical Theory of Management. He argued that any individual who performed these five functions could be considered a manager, regardless of his or her actual job title.

59. D: According to the National Environmental Policy Act of 1967, a business is required to prepare an environmental impact statement (EIS) when it builds a new factory, but not when it hires a new worker, makes a charitable contribution, or develops a new marketing initiative. Environmental impact statements assess the possible environmental concerns and damage that could result from a proposed action. Hiring new workers, making charitable contributions, and even developing marketing initiatives may be important decisions from a business perspective, but they are unlikely to have any major negative impact on the environment, and thus are exempted from the EIS requirement.

60. C: A manufacturing company that implements anti-pollution measures as outlined by applicable legislation, but that opts not to introduce any additional anti-pollution measures, has most likely adopted the Social Obligation Approach to business-society relations. This means that the business will follow all applicable laws, but will not make any supplemental attempts to improve the environment or contribute to social welfare. This model is based upon cost-benefit calculations, but such calculations are not an approach to business-society relations in and of themselves. The Social Responsibility and Social Responsiveness approaches denote moderate and high levels of social involvement, respectively.

61. D: A binding contract is an agreement signed and dated by both parties, and a witness.

62. B: This situation may constitute a violation of antitrust law. If the only two oil refiners in the U.S. merged, this would mean that there would be only one oil refiner in the U.S., thus creating a monopoly. Monopolies are generally illegal because they eliminate competition that ensures fair prices for consumers.

63. C: The Equal Employment Opportunity Commission (EEOC) is responsible for enforcing Civil Rights Act of 1964, the Equal Pay Act, and the Americans with Disabilities Act, but not the Environmental Protection Act. The EEOC is primarily responsible for enforcing civil rights, while the Environmental Protection Administration (EPA) is responsible for enforcing environmental protection statutes.

64. C: Anna would need word processing software, an Internet connection, and 1-5 GB of memory. Word processing software would allow Anna to compose simple fliers and advertising materials, and an Internet connection would allow Anna to communicate with clients via email and order supplies online. 1-5 GB of memory is what standard home and small business computers need, and Quickbooks is a type of accounting software that may be useful for Anna, but would not be necessary for the tasks listed in this question.

65. D: Microsoft Excel would most likely be used to analyze numerical sales data. This software program allows users to apply mathematical formulas to numerical and categorical data. While it does also produce charts and graphs that may ultimately be used in a sales presentation, such a presentation would probably be constructed using PowerPoint.

66. C: In order to prevent unauthorized individuals from accessing confidential data, a company might require a username and password to access its computer system, and also

construct a firewall to protect the computer system. By requiring passwords, the company can prevent unauthorized users such as former employees from accessing its computer system, and firewalls are designed to prevent hackers from accessing the data.

67. C: Employees may object to their social security numbers and birthdays being shared with others, and disclosing either of these could result in employee complaints and possible legal action. While information like name and work contact information must be shared in order for the business to function properly, information like Social Security numbers and birthdays is not relevant to the business, and thus should not be shared without employees' consent.

68. C: If a business education teacher has allotted one class period to help students identify potential career options, the most appropriate activity given these circumstances would be to administer a test that advises students about what careers might fit their interests and talents. While an internship might be useful, this would not fit the allotted time period. The other two options, describing a parent's job and describing a "dream job," may also be useful. However, they are not personalized, and they do not provide students with new options that he or she may not have considered before.

69. D: Real estate agents, insurance salespeople, and financial advisors all have extensive interaction with the public and require excellent people skills. Such jobs would not be suitable for those with an aversion to working with the public.

70. D: The four most important parts of a resume are the applicant's contact information, objective, educational attainment, and relevant work experience. The contact information is crucial because it allows the employer to get in touch with the applicant, and the objective is important because it explains why the applicant is sending the resume, and what position the applicant hopes to obtain. Educational attainment and work experience are important credentials for any job, while salary requirements and employment references are typically provided in the cover letter or upon request.

71. C: The most effective way to convey information about monthly stock gains and losses over a one-year period would be to use a line graph, which would clearly indicate month-to-month changes in stock price over time. Bar and pie charts are most effective for conveying categorical information about things like market share and sector weighting, and scatter plots are usually used to show results that are comprised of many individual responses, like survey results.

72. D: When manually proofreading documents, the correct way to indicate that a section of text should be removed is to draw a horizontal line through the text with a loop at the right end. Carets are used to indicate that something should be inserted into the text, and diagonal lines are used to indicate that a letter should be lower case instead of capitalized. Xs are not standard proofreading marks.

73. D: When researching a presentation about a national shipping business, the most detailed and comprehensive source of information about the top management of the company and its competitors would most likely be Hoovers.com. LexisNexis.com is also useful for business research, but it is a searchable database of academic and news articles, rather than a database of information about specific companies and industries, like Hoovers. The local newspaper or library would be unlikely to have detailed information

about competitors across the country, although it may have specific information about those located in the immediate vicinity.

74. C: Quicken, PeopleSoft, and Microsoft Office are all types of computer software. Quicken is used by individuals and small businesses for basic accounting functions, PeopleSoft is used primarily by human resources professionals, and Microsoft Office is the most widely-used word processing software on the market. The Internet is not a type of software, because it is not a program that can be installed and run on a single computer's operating system. The monitor, mouse, motherboard, and keyboard are all hardware, or equipment which is required to make software usable.

75. B: Search engine optimization (SEO) is the process of designing a website to maximize its placement in search engine results for particular keywords, thus increasing traffic to the site. Modifications are made to the website in order to make it highly relevant to certain search keywords, so that it will be among the first results Internet users see when they search for the designated keyword. This marketing tactic increases traffic to the website, and should increase sales on that website as well.

76. D: Links are used in all of the ways described here, except that they do not allow computer users to open software programs on their PC. In order to do that, one would click on an icon on one's own PC. Links, on the other hand, are inserted into a website's source code in such a way that clicking on them leads the Internet user to another website or webpage within the same site.

77. B: When designing a website for an online business, the web developer would include a site map in order to provide website users with a list of links to all of the pages on the website. Site maps, also called indexes, list each webpage that is part of the website.

78. D: Better Business Bureau certification is useful for businesses that engage in e-commerce because it reassures customers that the company is reliable and not trying to scam them. Better Business Bureau certification does not carry tax or legal protection, and the Better Business Bureau is not a governmental agency. Instead, it is a group of dues-paying members that are committed to setting and enforcing honest business practices.

79. D: Businesses can increase the security of confidential customer information by destroying paper records of credit card information, conducting employee background checks, and installing firewall and virus protection software to protect their computer systems. Firewalls and virus protection software prevent the theft of information stored on computers, and shredding paper records prevents theft as well. By conducting background checks prior to hiring employees, businesses can prevent theft by screening for individuals who have committed information or identity theft in the past.

80. D: A high school student who expresses interest in starting her own auto repair business after graduating from high school could best prepare for such a career by getting an internship or part time job at an auto-repair shop and by taking small business finance, law, and accounting courses. While experience and a basic understanding of how to run a small business would be crucial for success, a college degree and MBA would not be appropriate because they would not provide the student with the necessary industry experience she would need to be successful.

81. A: The best way for a business education teacher to evaluate her program in terms of how well graduates are prepared for the workforce would be to consult with local business leaders to find out where graduates have room for improvement. Asking students to complete internships would help prepare students for the workforce, but it would not provide the necessary feedback on students' preparedness. Surveying recent graduates would be useful, but it would provide less direct and detailed information about their performance in the workforce. Last, community college professors would be more familiar with students' performance in college courses than their performance in the workplace.

82. A: Of the activities listed here, the most effective tool for teaching business skills would be raising funds by selling concessions at athletic events. This would teach students how to attain permits and licenses, purchase and price inventory, develop a supply process, schedule employees, provide customer service, and account for sales, among many other functions that are necessary for running a small business. The other activities listed here would teach important skills, but fundraisers teach skills most directly relevant to business.

83. B: A business education teacher who is asked to serve as an advisor the local chapter of a student leadership organization is most likely to be responsible for ensuring the health and safety of student participants in the organization. In order to teach leadership and business skills, students are usually primarily responsible for holding meetings, planning activities, and accounting for funds. Advisors are present to guide students and protect students' health and safety.

84. C: A business education teacher and a math teacher coordinating their lesson plans so that the concepts taught in math class are subsequently applied to real situations in the business class is the best example of interdisciplinary collaboration. While the other examples do require students to use skills learned in other classes like math and language arts, only example B involves active coordination between teachers in two different subject areas.

85. D: The activity that would most effectively and comprehensively assess how well students have mastered learning objectives for a unit about small business would be writing and presenting a business plan. While marketing is an important aspect of running a small business, developing a business plan would more comprehensively and directly measure and reinforce students' knowledge about small businesses.

86. D: All of the activities described here would teach skills that are necessary for working in a culturally diverse workplace. Students need to know the legal rights and responsibilities of employees and employers vis-à-vis this issue. They should also understand the perspectives of people from culturally diverse backgrounds, as well the unique problems they face in the workplace.

87. C: Based upon the information in Table 2, the correct order for the list is Business D, Business C, Business A, Business B. The triple A rating indicates the least risk, followed by double A, triple B, and double B.

88. C: If Scott Smith is paid $10 per hour on weekdays and $11 per hour on weekends, he worked a total of 16 weekday hours for $160 and 4 weekend hours for $44, for a total of $204.00.

89. C: Smith, who is a part time employee, should have social security, Medicare, and income taxes deducted from his check, because he is a W-4 employee. Since he worked less than 40 hours from November 1st through November 7th, though, he is not a full time employee and does not have health insurance or 401k deductions.

90. B: If Scott contributes 4% of his $2,000 paycheck to his 401k, this would total $80 per pay period, and the company would have to match 100% of this contribution, which would be $80.

91. C: Accounts receivable are current assets, also known as short-term assets. This term refers to open accounts that are not yet due. For example, if a landscaping company mows Anna's lawn today and the company sends her a bill for the service that is due one month later, then Anna's account would be in "account receivable" status until the due date.

92. D: Owners' equity is comprised of the amount of their initial investment in the business plus any unclaimed profits from the business' operation. (Unclaimed profits are also called retained earnings).

93. C: According to the Copyright Act of 1976, creative works like plays, poems, and architectural plans are protected by copyright law so long as they are written down. Advertising slogans are not protected because they fall under the jurisdiction of trademark law.

94. A: A phrase that is associated with a particular product would be protected by trademark law. Copyright law protects creative work, while trademarks protect business-related slogans, symbols, etc., which distinguish one product from another.

95. A: A corporation is always owned by shareholders. This means that the corporation is a separate legal entity from its shareholders. As a consequence of this, shareholders' only personal financial risk is their investment. They, unlike the corporation itself, cannot be sued by debtors if the company fails.

96. B: If an employee becomes injured because an employer did not provide equipment in good working order, this would be an example of an OSHA violation by the employer. Employees are allowed to work in hazardous conditions, so long as the employer provides adequate safety protection. Employers have the right to accompany an OSHA compliance officer on an inspection, but they are not required to do so. Employees are not covered by the OSHA act during normal commutes to and from work.

97. D: "The employee will have excellent writing skills" states the desired qualification clearly and correctly. "The employee, will have excellent oral communication skills" is incorrect because the comma is unnecessary. In the second sentence, "employee's" is possessive, and should have an apostrophe (employees'). In the third sentence, the word "well" is an adverb that would be best placed next to the verb which it modifies ("communicate well" would be correct).

98. C: The Internet is an example of a Wide Area Network (WAN). WANs are networks that cover an extremely large area. LANs (local area networks) cover smaller areas, like offices. LANs usually have faster data transfer speeds than WANs.

99. D: Nothing can be concluded from these results because students' baseline performance on these tests was not measured before the experiment. It is possible that one group of students already knew more about business, or were more academically advanced to start with. In order to account for this possibility, each group of students should have been tested prior to the beginning of the class. The effectiveness of the two teaching methods could then be compared based on the change in students' scores between the first and second test administrations.

100. C: It is illegal to employ someone under 18 in a job deemed hazardous. Such jobs include mining and manufacturing. Youths aged 16 and 17 can work in any job that is not hazardous, and youths under 14 can work in certain designated jobs like newspaper delivery and babysitting. In cases were state and federal laws conflict, the law that is more protective of minors takes precedence.

Secret Key #1 - Time is Your Greatest Enemy

Pace Yourself

Wear a watch. At the beginning of the test, check the time (or start a chronometer on your watch to count the minutes), and check the time after every few questions to make sure you are "on schedule."

If you are forced to speed up, do it efficiently. Usually one or more answer choices can be eliminated without too much difficulty. Above all, don't panic. Don't speed up and just begin guessing at random choices. By pacing yourself, and continually monitoring your progress against your watch, you will always know exactly how far ahead or behind you are with your available time. If you find that you are one minute behind on the test, don't skip one question without spending any time on it, just to catch back up. Take 15 fewer seconds on the next four questions, and after four questions you'll have caught back up. Once you catch back up, you can continue working each problem at your normal pace.

Furthermore, don't dwell on the problems that you were rushed on. If a problem was taking up too much time and you made a hurried guess, it must be difficult. The difficult questions are the ones you are most likely to miss anyway, so it isn't a big loss. It is better to end with more time than you need than to run out of time.

Lastly, sometimes it is beneficial to slow down if you are constantly getting ahead of time. You are always more likely to catch a careless mistake by working more slowly than quickly, and among very high-scoring test takers (those who are likely to have lots of time left over), careless errors affect the score more than mastery of material.

Secret Key #2 - Guessing is not Guesswork

You probably know that guessing is a good idea. Unlike other standardized tests, there is no penalty for getting a wrong answer. Even if you have no idea about a question, you still have a 20-25% chance of getting it right.

Most test takers do not understand the impact that proper guessing can have on their score. Unless you score extremely high, guessing will significantly contribute to your final score.

Monkeys Take the Test

What most test takers don't realize is that to insure that 20-25% chance, you have to guess randomly. If you put 20 monkeys in a room to take this test, assuming they answered once per question and behaved themselves, on average they would get 20-25% of the questions correct. Put 20 test takers in the room, and the average will be much lower among guessed questions. Why?

1. The test writers intentionally write deceptive answer choices that "look" right. A test taker has no idea about a question, so he picks the "best looking" answer, which is often wrong. The monkey has no idea what looks good and what doesn't, so it will consistently be right about 20-25% of the time.
2. Test takers will eliminate answer choices from the guessing pool based on a hunch or intuition. Simple but correct answers often get excluded, leaving a 0% chance of being correct. The monkey has no clue, and often gets lucky with the best choice.

This is why the process of elimination endorsed by most test courses is flawed and detrimental to your performance. Test takers don't guess; they make an ignorant stab in the dark that is usually worse than random.

$5 Challenge

Let me introduce one of the most valuable ideas of this course—the $5 challenge:

You only mark your "best guess" if you are willing to bet $5 on it.
You only eliminate choices from guessing if you are willing to bet $5 on it.

Why $5? Five dollars is an amount of money that is small yet not insignificant, and can really add up fast (20 questions could cost you $100). Likewise, each answer choice on one question of the test will have a small impact on your overall score, but it can really add up to a lot of points in the end.

The process of elimination IS valuable. The following shows your chance of guessing it right:

If you eliminate wrong answer choices until only this many remain:	Chance of getting it correct:
1	100%
2	50%
3	33%

However, if you accidentally eliminate the right answer or go on a hunch for an incorrect answer, your chances drop dramatically—to 0%. By guessing among all the answer choices, you are GUARANTEED to have a shot at the right answer.

That's why the $5 test is so valuable. If you give up the advantage and safety of a pure guess, it had better be worth the risk.

What we still haven't covered is how to be sure that whatever guess you make is truly random. Here's the easiest way:

Always pick the first answer choice among those remaining.

Such a technique means that you have decided, **before you see a single test question**, exactly how you are going to guess, and since the order of choices tells you nothing about which one is correct, this guessing technique is perfectly random.

This section is not meant to scare you away from making educated guesses or eliminating choices; you just need to define when a choice is worth eliminating. The $5 test, along with a pre-defined random guessing strategy, is the best way to make sure you reap all of the benefits of guessing.

Secret Key #3 - Practice Smarter, Not Harder

Many test takers delay the test preparation process because they dread the awful amounts of practice time they think necessary to succeed on the test. We have refined an effective method that will take you only a fraction of the time.

There are a number of "obstacles" in the path to success. Among these are answering questions, finishing in time, and mastering test-taking strategies. All must be executed on the day of the test at peak performance, or your score will suffer. The test is a mental marathon that has a large impact on your future.

Just like a marathon runner, it is important to work your way up to the full challenge. So first you just worry about questions, and then time, and finally strategy:

Success Strategy

1. Find a good source for practice tests.
2. If you are willing to make a larger time investment, consider using more than one study guide. Often the different approaches of multiple authors will help you "get" difficult concepts.
3. Take a practice test with no time constraints, with all study helps, "open book." Take your time with questions and focus on applying strategies.
4. Take a practice test with time constraints, with all guides, "open book."
5. Take a final practice test without open material and with time limits.

If you have time to take more practice tests, just repeat step 5. By gradually exposing yourself to the full rigors of the test environment, you will condition your mind to the stress of test day and maximize your success.

Secret Key #4 - Prepare, Don't Procrastinate

Let me state an obvious fact: if you take the test three times, you will probably get three different scores. This is due to the way you feel on test day, the level of preparedness you have, and the version of the test you see. Despite the test writers' claims to the contrary, some versions of the test WILL be easier for you than others.

Since your future depends so much on your score, you should maximize your chances of success. In order to maximize the likelihood of success, you've got to prepare in advance. This means taking practice tests and spending time learning the information and test taking strategies you will need to succeed.

Never go take the actual test as a "practice" test, expecting that you can just take it again if you need to. Take all the practice tests you can on your own, but when you go to take the official test, be prepared, be focused, and do your best the first time!

Secret Key #5 - Test Yourself

Everyone knows that time is money. There is no need to spend too much of your time or too little of your time preparing for the test. You should only spend as much of your precious time preparing as is necessary for you to get the score you need.

Once you have taken a practice test under real conditions of time constraints, then you will know if you are ready for the test or not.

If you have scored extremely high the first time that you take the practice test, then there is not much point in spending countless hours studying. You are already there.

Benchmark your abilities by retaking practice tests and seeing how much you have improved. Once you consistently score high enough to guarantee success, then you are ready.

If you have scored well below where you need, then knuckle down and begin studying in earnest. Check your improvement regularly through the use of practice tests under real conditions. Above all, don't worry, panic, or give up. The key is perseverance!

Then, when you go to take the test, remain confident and remember how well you did on the practice tests. If you can score high enough on a practice test, then you can do the same on the real thing.

General Strategies

The most important thing you can do is to ignore your fears and jump into the test immediately. Do not be overwhelmed by any strange-sounding terms. You have to jump into the test like jumping into a pool—all at once is the easiest way.

Make Predictions

As you read and understand the question, try to guess what the answer will be. Remember that several of the answer choices are wrong, and once you begin reading them, your mind will immediately become cluttered with answer choices designed to throw you off. Your mind is typically the most focused immediately after you have read the question and digested its contents. If you can, try to predict what the correct answer will be. You may be surprised at what you can predict.

Quickly scan the choices and see if your prediction is in the listed answer choices. If it is, then you can be quite confident that you have the right answer. It still won't hurt to check the other answer choices, but most of the time, you've got it!

Answer the Question

It may seem obvious to only pick answer choices that answer the question, but the test writers can create some excellent answer choices that are wrong. Don't pick an answer just because it sounds right, or you believe it to be true. It MUST answer the question. Once you've made your selection, always go back and check it against the question and make sure that you didn't misread the question and that the answer choice does answer the question posed.

Benchmark

After you read the first answer choice, decide if you think it sounds correct or not. If it doesn't, move on to the next answer choice. If it does, mentally mark that answer choice. This doesn't mean that you've definitely selected it as your answer choice, it just means that it's the best you've seen thus far. Go ahead and read the next choice. If the next choice is worse than the one you've already selected, keep going to the next answer choice. If the next choice is better than the choice you've already selected, mentally mark the new answer choice as your best guess.

The first answer choice that you select becomes your standard. Every other answer choice must be benchmarked against that standard. That choice is correct until proven otherwise by another answer choice beating it out. Once you've decided that no other answer choice seems as good, do one final check to ensure that your answer choice answers the question posed.

Valid Information

Don't discount any of the information provided in the question. Every piece of information may be necessary to determine the correct answer. None of the information in the question is there to throw you off (while the answer choices will certainly have information to throw you off). If two seemingly unrelated topics are discussed, don't ignore either. You can be confident there is a relationship, or it wouldn't be included in the question, and you are probably going to have to determine what is that relationship to find the answer.

Avoid "Fact Traps"

Don't get distracted by a choice that is factually true. Your search is for the answer that answers the question. Stay focused and don't fall for an answer that is true but irrelevant. Always go back to the question and make sure you're choosing an answer that actually answers the question and is not just a true statement. An answer can be factually correct, but it MUST answer the question asked. Additionally, two answers can both be seemingly correct, so be sure to read all of the answer choices, and make sure that you get the one that BEST answers the question.

Milk the Question

Some of the questions may throw you completely off. They might deal with a subject you have not been exposed to, or one that you haven't reviewed in years. While your lack of knowledge about the subject will be a hindrance, the question itself can give you many clues that will help you find the correct answer. Read the question carefully and look for clues. Watch particularly for adjectives and nouns describing difficult terms or words that you don't recognize. Regardless of whether you completely understand a word or not, replacing it with a synonym, either provided or one you more familiar with, may help you to understand what the questions are asking. Rather than wracking your mind about specific detailed information concerning a difficult term or word, try to use mental substitutes that are easier to understand.

The Trap of Familiarity

Don't just choose a word because you recognize it. On difficult questions, you may not recognize a number of words in the answer choices. The test writers don't put "make-believe" words on the test, so don't think that just because you only recognize all the words in one answer choice that that answer choice must be correct. If you only recognize words in one answer choice, then focus on that one. Is it correct? Try your best to determine if it is correct. If it is, that's great. If not, eliminate it. Each word and answer choice you eliminate increases your chances of getting the question correct, even if you then have to guess among the unfamiliar choices.

Eliminate Answers

Eliminate choices as soon as you realize they are wrong. But be careful! Make sure you consider all of the possible answer choices. Just because one appears right, doesn't mean that the next one won't be even better! The test writers will usually put more than one good answer choice for every question, so read all of them. Don't worry if you are stuck between two that seem right. By getting down to just two remaining possible choices, your odds are now 50/50. Rather than wasting too much time, play the odds. You are guessing, but guessing wisely because you've been able to knock out some of the answer choices that you know are wrong. If you are eliminating choices and realize that the last answer choice you are left with is also obviously wrong, don't panic. Start over and consider each choice again. There may easily be something that you missed the first time and will realize on the second pass.

Tough Questions

If you are stumped on a problem or it appears too hard or too difficult, don't waste time. Move on! Remember though, if you can quickly check for obviously incorrect answer choices, your chances of guessing correctly are greatly improved. Before you completely give up, at least try to knock out a couple of possible answers. Eliminate what you can and then guess at the remaining answer choices before moving on.

Brainstorm

If you get stuck on a difficult question, spend a few seconds quickly brainstorming. Run through the complete list of possible answer choices. Look at each choice and ask yourself, "Could this answer the question satisfactorily?" Go through each answer choice and consider it independently of the others. By systematically going through all possibilities, you may find something that you would otherwise overlook. Remember though that when you get stuck, it's important to try to keep moving.

Read Carefully

Understand the problem. Read the question and answer choices carefully. Don't miss the question because you misread the terms. You have plenty of time to read each question thoroughly and make sure you understand what is being asked. Yet a happy medium must be attained, so don't waste too much time. You must read carefully, but efficiently.

Face Value

When in doubt, use common sense. Always accept the situation in the problem at face value. Don't read too much into it. These problems will not require you to make huge leaps of logic. The test writers aren't trying to throw you off with a cheap trick. If you have to go beyond creativity and make a leap of logic in order to have an answer choice answer the question, then you should look at the other answer choices. Don't overcomplicate the problem by creating theoretical relationships or explanations that will warp time or space. These are normal problems rooted in reality. It's just that the applicable relationship or explanation may not be readily apparent and you have to figure things out. Use your common sense to interpret anything that isn't clear.

Prefixes

If you're having trouble with a word in the question or answer choices, try dissecting it. Take advantage of every clue that the word might include. Prefixes and suffixes can be a huge help. Usually they allow you to determine a basic meaning. Pre- means before, post-means after, pro - is positive, de- is negative. From these prefixes and suffixes, you can get an idea of the general meaning of the word and try to put it into context. Beware though of any traps. Just because con- is the opposite of pro-, doesn't necessarily mean congress is the opposite of progress!

Hedge Phrases

Watch out for critical hedge phrases, led off with words such as "likely," "may," "can," "sometimes," "often," "almost," "mostly," "usually," "generally," "rarely," and "sometimes." Question writers insert these hedge phrases to cover every possibility. Often an answer choice will be wrong simply because it leaves no room for exception. Unless the situation calls for them, avoid answer choices that have definitive words like "exactly," and "always."

Switchback Words

Stay alert for "switchbacks." These are the words and phrases frequently used to alert you to shifts in thought. The most common switchback word is "but." Others include "although," "however," "nevertheless," "on the other hand," "even though," "while," "in spite of," "despite," and "regardless of."

New Information

Correct answer choices will rarely have completely new information included. Answer choices typically are straightforward reflections of the material asked about and will directly relate to the question. If a new piece of information is included in an answer choice that doesn't even seem to relate to the topic being asked about, then that answer choice is likely incorrect. All of the information needed to answer the question is usually provided for you in the question. You should not have to make guesses that are unsupported or choose answer choices that require unknown information that cannot be reasoned from what is given.

Time Management

On technical questions, don't get lost on the technical terms. Don't spend too much time on any one question. If you don't know what a term means, then odds are you aren't going to get much further since you don't have a dictionary. You should be able to immediately recognize whether or not you know a term. If you don't, work with the other clues that you have—the other answer choices and terms provided—but don't waste too much time trying to figure out a difficult term that you don't know.

Contextual Clues

Look for contextual clues. An answer can be right but not the correct answer. The contextual clues will help you find the answer that is most right and is correct. Understand the context in which a phrase or statement is made. This will help you make important distinctions.

Don't Panic

Panicking will not answer any questions for you; therefore, it isn't helpful. When you first see the question, if your mind goes blank, take a deep breath. Force yourself to mechanically go through the steps of solving the problem using the strategies you've learned.

Pace Yourself

Don't get clock fever. It's easy to be overwhelmed when you're looking at a page full of questions, your mind is full of random thoughts and feeling confused, and the clock is ticking down faster than you would like. Calm down and maintain the pace that you have set for yourself. As long as you are on track by monitoring your pace, you are guaranteed to have enough time for yourself. When you get to the last few minutes of the test, it may seem like you won't have enough time left, but if you only have as many questions as you should have left at that point, then you're right on track!

Answer Selection

The best way to pick an answer choice is to eliminate all of those that are wrong, until only one is left and confirm that is the correct answer. Sometimes though, an answer choice may immediately look right. Be careful! Take a second to make sure that the other choices are not equally obvious. Don't make a hasty mistake. There are only two times that you should stop before checking other answers. First is when you are positive that the answer choice you have selected is correct. Second is when time is almost out and you have to make a quick guess!

Check Your Work

Since you will probably not know every term listed and the answer to every question, it is important that you get credit for the ones that you do know. Don't miss any questions through careless mistakes. If at all possible, try to take a second to look back over your answer selection and make sure you've selected the correct answer choice and haven't made a costly careless mistake (such as marking an answer choice that you didn't mean to mark). The time it takes for this quick double check should more than pay for itself in caught mistakes.

Beware of Directly Quoted Answers

Sometimes an answer choice will repeat word for word a portion of the question or reference section. However, beware of such exact duplication. It may be a trap! More than likely, the correct choice will paraphrase or summarize a point, rather than being exactly the same wording.

Slang

Scientific sounding answers are better than slang ones. An answer choice that begins "To compare the outcomes..." is much more likely to be correct than one that begins "Because some people insisted..."

Extreme Statements

Avoid wild answers that throw out highly controversial ideas that are proclaimed as established fact. An answer choice that states the "process should used in certain situations, if..." is much more likely to be correct than one that states the "process should be discontinued completely." The first is a calm rational statement and doesn't even make a definitive, uncompromising stance, using a hedge word "if" to provide wiggle room, whereas the second choice is a radical idea and far more extreme.

Answer Choice Families

When you have two or more answer choices that are direct opposites or parallels, one of them is usually the correct answer. For instance, if one answer choice states "x increases" and another answer choice states "x decreases" or "y increases," then those two or three answer choices are very similar in construction and fall into the same family of answer choices. A family of answer choices consists of two or three answer choices, very similar in construction, but often with directly opposite meanings. Usually the correct answer choice will be in that family of answer choices. The "odd man out" or answer choice that doesn't seem to fit the parallel construction of the other answer choices is more likely to be incorrect.

Special Report: How to Overcome Test Anxiety

The very nature of tests caters to some level of anxiety, nervousness, or tension, just as we feel for any important event that occurs in our lives. A little bit of anxiety or nervousness can be a good thing. It helps us with motivation, and makes achievement just that much sweeter. However, too much anxiety can be a problem, especially if it hinders our ability to function and perform.

"Test anxiety," is the term that refers to the emotional reactions that some test-takers experience when faced with a test or exam. Having a fear of testing and exams is based upon a rational fear, since the test-taker's performance can shape the course of an academic career. Nevertheless, experiencing excessive fear of examinations will only interfere with the test-taker's ability to perform and chance to be successful.

There are a large variety of causes that can contribute to the development and sensation of test anxiety. These include, but are not limited to, lack of preparation and worrying about issues surrounding the test.

Lack of Preparation

Lack of preparation can be identified by the following behaviors or situations:

Not scheduling enough time to study, and therefore cramming the night before the test or exam
Managing time poorly, to create the sensation that there is not enough time to do everything
Failing to organize the text information in advance, so that the study material consists of the entire text and not simply the pertinent information
Poor overall studying habits

Worrying, on the other hand, can be related to both the test taker, or many other factors around him/her that will be affected by the results of the test. These include worrying about:

Previous performances on similar exams, or exams in general
How friends and other students are achieving
The negative consequences that will result from a poor grade or failure

There are three primary elements to test anxiety. Physical components, which involve the same typical bodily reactions as those to acute anxiety (to be discussed below). Emotional factors have to do with fear or panic. Mental or cognitive issues concerning attention spans and memory abilities.

Physical Signals

There are many different symptoms of test anxiety, and these are not limited to mental and emotional strain. Frequently there are a range of physical signals that will let a test taker know that he/she is suffering from test anxiety. These bodily changes can include the following:

Perspiring
Sweaty palms
Wet, trembling hands
Nausea
Dry mouth
A knot in the stomach
Headache
Faintness
Muscle tension
Aching shoulders, back and neck
Rapid heart beat
Feeling too hot/cold

To recognize the sensation of test anxiety, a test-taker should monitor him/herself for the following sensations:

The physical distress symptoms as listed above
Emotional sensitivity, expressing emotional feelings such as the need to cry or laugh too much, or a sensation of anger or helplessness
A decreased ability to think, causing the test-taker to blank out or have racing thoughts that are hard to organize or control.

Though most students will feel some level of anxiety when faced with a test or exam, the majority can cope with that anxiety and maintain it at a manageable level. However, those who cannot are faced with a very real and very serious condition, which can and should be controlled for the immeasurable benefit of this sufferer.

Naturally, these sensations lead to negative results for the testing experience. The most common effects of test anxiety have to do with nervousness and mental blocking.

Nervousness

Nervousness can appear in several different levels:

The test-taker's difficulty, or even inability to read and understand the questions on the test
The difficulty or inability to organize thoughts to a coherent form
The difficulty or inability to recall key words and concepts relating to the testing questions (especially essays)
The receipt of poor grades on a test, though the test material was well known by the test taker

Conversely, a person may also experience mental blocking, which involves:

Blanking out on test questions
Only remembering the correct answers to the questions when the test has already finished.

Fortunately for test anxiety sufferers, beating these feelings, to a large degree, has to do with proper preparation. When a test taker has a feeling of preparedness, then anxiety will be dramatically lessened.

The first step to resolving anxiety issues is to distinguish which of the two types of anxiety are being suffered. If the anxiety is a direct result of a lack of preparation, this should be considered a normal reaction, and the anxiety level (as opposed to the test results) shouldn't be anything to worry about. However, if, when adequately prepared, the test-taker still panics, blanks out, or seems to overreact, this is not a fully rational reaction. While this can be considered normal too, there are many ways to combat and overcome these effects.

Remember that anxiety cannot be entirely eliminated, however, there are ways to minimize it, to make the anxiety easier to manage. Preparation is one of the best ways to minimize test anxiety. Therefore the following techniques are wise in order to best fight off any anxiety that may want to build.

To begin with, try to avoid cramming before a test, whenever it is possible. By trying to memorize an entire term's worth of information in one day, you'll be shocking your system, and not giving yourself a very good chance to absorb the information. This is an easy path to anxiety, so for those who suffer from test anxiety, cramming should not even be considered an option.

Instead of cramming, work throughout the semester to combine all of the material which is presented throughout the semester, and work on it gradually as the course goes by, making sure to master the main concepts first, leaving minor details for a week or so before the test.

To study for the upcoming exam, be sure to pose questions that may be on the examination, to gauge the ability to answer them by integrating the ideas from your texts, notes and lectures, as well as any supplementary readings.

If it is truly impossible to cover all of the information that was covered in that particular term, concentrate on the most important portions, that can be covered very well. Learn these concepts as best as possible, so that when the test comes, a goal can be made to use these concepts as presentations of your knowledge.

In addition to study habits, changes in attitude are critical to beating a struggle with test anxiety. In fact, an improvement of the perspective over the entire test-taking experience can actually help a test taker to enjoy studying and therefore improve the overall experience. Be certain not to overemphasize the significance of the grade - know that the result of the test is neither a reflection of self worth, nor is it a measure of intelligence; one grade will not predict a person's future success.

To improve an overall testing outlook, the following steps should be tried:

Keeping in mind that the most reasonable expectation for taking a test is to expect to try to demonstrate as much of what you know as you possibly can.
Reminding ourselves that a test is only one test; this is not the only one, and there will be others.
The thought of thinking of oneself in an irrational, all-or-nothing term should be avoided at all costs.
A reward should be designated for after the test, so there's something to look forward to. Whether it be going to a movie, going out to eat, or simply visiting friends, schedule it in advance, and do it no matter what result is expected on the exam.

Test-takers should also keep in mind that the basics are some of the most important things, even beyond anti-anxiety techniques and studying. Never neglect the basic social, emotional and biological needs, in order to try to absorb information. In order to best achieve, these three factors must be held as just as important as the studying itself.

Study Steps

Remember the following important steps for studying:

Maintain healthy nutrition and exercise habits. Continue both your recreational activities and social pass times. These both contribute to your physical and emotional well being.
Be certain to get a good amount of sleep, especially the night before the test, because when you're overtired you are not able to perform to the best of your best ability.
Keep the studying pace to a moderate level by taking breaks when they are needed, and varying the work whenever possible, to keep the mind fresh instead of getting bored.
When enough studying has been done that all the material that can be learned has been learned, and the test taker is prepared for the test, stop studying and do something relaxing such as listening to music, watching a movie, or taking a warm bubble bath.

There are also many other techniques to minimize the uneasiness or apprehension that is experienced along with test anxiety before, during, or even after the examination. In fact, there are a great deal of things that can be done to stop anxiety from interfering with lifestyle and performance. Again, remember that anxiety will not be eliminated entirely, and it shouldn't be. Otherwise that "up" feeling for exams would not exist, and most of us depend on that sensation to perform better than usual. However, this anxiety has to be at a level that is manageable.

Of course, as we have just discussed, being prepared for the exam is half the battle right away. Attending all classes, finding out what knowledge will be expected on the exam, and knowing the exam schedules are easy steps to lowering anxiety. Keeping up with work will remove the need to cram, and efficient study habits will eliminate wasted time. Studying should be done in an ideal location for concentration, so that it is simple to become interested in the material and give it complete attention. A method such as SQ3R (Survey, Question, Read, Recite, Review) is a wonderful key to follow to make sure that the study habits are as effective as possible, especially in the case of learning from a textbook. Flashcards are great techniques for memorization. Learning to take good notes will mean that notes will be full of useful information, so that less sifting will need to be done to seek out what is pertinent for studying. Reviewing notes after class and then again on occasion will keep the information fresh in the mind. From notes that have been taken summary sheets and outlines can be made for simpler reviewing.

A study group can also be a very motivational and helpful place to study, as there will be a sharing of ideas, all of the minds can work together, to make sure that everyone understands, and the studying will be made more interesting because it will be a social occasion.

Basically, though, as long as the test-taker remains organized and self confident, with efficient study habits, less time will need to be spent studying, and higher grades will be achieved.

To become self confident, there are many useful steps. The first of these is "self talk." It has been shown through extensive research, that self-talk for students who suffer from test anxiety, should be well monitored, in order to make sure that it contributes to self confidence as opposed to sinking the student. Frequently the self talk of test-anxious students is negative or self-defeating, thinking that everyone else is smarter and faster, that they always mess up, and that if they don't do well, they'll fail the entire course. It is important to decreasing anxiety that awareness is made of self talk. Try writing any negative self thoughts and then disputing them with a positive statement instead. Begin self-encouragement as though it was a friend speaking. Repeat positive statements to help reprogram the mind to believing in successes instead of failures.

Helpful Techniques

Other extremely helpful techniques include:

Self-visualization of doing well and reaching goals
While aiming for an "A" level of understanding, don't try to "overprotect" by setting your expectations lower. This will only convince the mind to stop studying in order to meet the lower expectations.
Don't make comparisons with the results or habits of other students. These are individual factors, and different things work for different people, causing different results.
Strive to become an expert in learning what works well, and what can be done in order to improve. Consider collecting this data in a journal.
Create rewards for after studying instead of doing things before studying that will only turn into avoidance behaviors.
Make a practice of relaxing - by using methods such as progressive relaxation, self-hypnosis, guided imagery, etc - in order to make relaxation an automatic sensation.
Work on creating a state of relaxed concentration so that concentrating will take on the focus of the mind, so that none will be wasted on worrying.
Take good care of the physical self by eating well and getting enough sleep.
Plan in time for exercise and stick to this plan.

Beyond these techniques, there are other methods to be used before, during and after the test that will help the test-taker perform well in addition to overcoming anxiety.

Before the exam comes the academic preparation. This involves establishing a study schedule and beginning at least one week before the actual date of the test. By doing this, the anxiety of not having enough time to study for the test will be automatically eliminated. Moreover, this will make the studying a much more effective experience, ensuring that the learning will be an easier process. This relieves much undue pressure on the test-taker.

Summary sheets, note cards, and flash cards with the main concepts and examples of these main concepts should be prepared in advance of the actual studying time. A topic should never be eliminated from this process. By omitting a topic because it isn't expected to be on the test is only setting up the test-taker for anxiety should it actually appear on the exam. Utilize the course syllabus for laying out the topics that should be studied. Carefully go over the notes that were made in class, paying special attention to any of the issues that the professor took special care to emphasize while lecturing in class. In the textbooks, use the chapter review, or if possible, the chapter tests, to begin your review.

It may even be possible to ask the instructor what information will be covered on the exam, or what the format of the exam will be (for example, multiple choice, essay, free form, true-false). Additionally, see if it is possible to find out how many questions will be on the test. If a review sheet or sample test has been offered by the professor, make good use of it, above anything else, for the preparation for the test. Another great resource for getting to know the examination is reviewing tests from previous semesters. Use these tests to review, and aim to achieve a 100% score on each of the possible topics. With a few exceptions, the goal that you set for yourself is the highest one that you will reach.

Take all of the questions that were assigned as homework, and rework them to any other possible course material. The more problems reworked, the more skill and confidence will form as a result. When forming the solution to a problem, write out each of the steps. Don't simply do head work. By doing as many steps on paper as possible, much clarification and therefore confidence will be formed. Do this with as many homework problems as possible, before checking the answers. By checking the answer after each problem, a reinforcement will exist, that will not be on the exam. Study situations should be as exam-like as possible, to prime the test-taker's system for the experience. By waiting to check the answers at the end, a psychological advantage will be formed, to decrease the stress factor.

Another fantastic reason for not cramming is the avoidance of confusion in concepts, especially when it comes to mathematics. 8-10 hours of study will become one hundred percent more effective if it is spread out over a week or at least several days, instead of doing it all in one sitting. Recognize that the human brain requires time in order to assimilate new material, so frequent breaks and a span of study time over several days will be much more beneficial.

Additionally, don't study right up until the point of the exam. Studying should stop a minimum of one hour before the exam begins. This allows the brain to rest and put things in their proper order. This will also provide the time to become as relaxed as possible when going into the examination room. The test-taker will also have time to eat well and eat sensibly. Know that the brain needs food as much as the rest of the body. With enough food and enough sleep, as well as a relaxed attitude, the body and the mind are primed for success.

Avoid any anxious classmates who are talking about the exam. These students only spread anxiety, and are not worth sharing the anxious sentimentalities.

Before the test also involves creating a positive attitude, so mental preparation should also be a point of concentration. There are many keys to creating a positive attitude. Should fears become rushing in, make a visualization of taking the exam, doing well, and seeing an A written on the paper. Write out a list of affirmations that will bring a feeling of confidence, such as "I am doing well in my English class," "I studied well and know my material," "I enjoy this class." Even if the affirmations aren't believed at first, it sends a positive message to the subconscious which will result in an alteration of the overall belief system, which is the system that creates reality.

If a sensation of panic begins, work with the fear and imagine the very worst! Work through the entire scenario of not passing the test, failing the entire course, and dropping out of school, followed by not getting a job, and pushing a shopping cart through the dark alley where you'll live. This will place things into perspective! Then, practice deep breathing and create a visualization of the opposite situation - achieving an "A" on the exam, passing the entire course, receiving the degree at a graduation ceremony.

On the day of the test, there are many things to be done to ensure the best results, as well as the most calm outlook. The following stages are suggested in order to maximize test-taking potential:

Begin the examination day with a moderate breakfast, and avoid any coffee or beverages with caffeine if the test taker is prone to jitters. Even people who are used to managing caffeine can feel jittery or light-headed when it is taken on a test day.
Attempt to do something that is relaxing before the examination begins. As last minute cramming clouds the mastering of overall concepts, it is better to use this time to create a calming outlook.
Be certain to arrive at the test location well in advance, in order to provide time to select a location that is away from doors, windows and other distractions, as well as giving enough time to relax before the test begins.
Keep away from anxiety generating classmates who will upset the sensation of stability and relaxation that is being attempted before the exam.
Should the waiting period before the exam begins cause anxiety, create a self-distraction by reading a light magazine or something else that is relaxing and simple.

During the exam itself, read the entire exam from beginning to end, and find out how much time should be allotted to each individual problem. Once writing the exam, should more time be taken for a problem, it should be abandoned, in order to begin another problem. If there is time at the end, the unfinished problem can always be returned to and completed.

Read the instructions very carefully - twice - so that unpleasant surprises won't follow during or after the exam has ended.

When writing the exam, pretend that the situation is actually simply the completion of homework within a library, or at home. This will assist in forming a relaxed atmosphere, and will allow the brain extra focus for the complex thinking function.

Begin the exam with all of the questions with which the most confidence is felt. This will build the confidence level regarding the entire exam and will begin a quality momentum. This will also create encouragement for trying the problems where uncertainty resides.

Going with the "gut instinct" is always the way to go when solving a problem. Second guessing should be avoided at all costs. Have confidence in the ability to do well.

For essay questions, create an outline in advance that will keep the mind organized and make certain that all of the points are remembered. For multiple choice, read every answer, even if the correct one has been spotted - a better one may exist.

Continue at a pace that is reasonable and not rushed, in order to be able to work carefully. Provide enough time to go over the answers at the end, to check for small errors that can be corrected.

Should a feeling of panic begin, breathe deeply, and think of the feeling of the body releasing sand through its pores. Visualize a calm, peaceful place, and include all of the sights, sounds and sensations of this image. Continue the deep breathing, and take a few minutes to continue this with closed eyes. When all is well again, return to the test.

If a "blanking" occurs for a certain question, skip it and move on to the next question. There will be time to return to the other question later. Get everything done that can be done, first, to guarantee all the grades that can be compiled, and to build all of the confidence possible. Then return to the weaker questions to build the marks from there.

Remember, one's own reality can be created, so as long as the belief is there, success will follow. And remember: anxiety can happen later, right now, there's an exam to be written!

After the examination is complete, whether there is a feeling for a good grade or a bad grade, don't dwell on the exam, and be certain to follow through on the reward that was promised...and enjoy it! Don't dwell on any mistakes that have been made, as there is nothing that can be done at this point anyway.

Additionally, don't begin to study for the next test right away. Do something relaxing for a while, and let the mind relax and prepare itself to begin absorbing information again.

From the results of the exam - both the grade and the entire experience, be certain to learn from what has gone on. Perfect studying habits and work some more on confidence in order to make the next examination experience even better than the last one.

Learn to avoid places where openings occurred for laziness, procrastination and day dreaming.

Use the time between this exam and the next one to better learn to relax, even learning to relax on cue, so that any anxiety can be controlled during the next exam. Learn how to relax the body. Slouch in your chair if that helps. Tighten and then relax all of the different muscle groups, one group at a time, beginning with the feet and then working all the way up to the neck and face. This will ultimately relax the muscles more than they were to begin with. Learn how to breathe deeply and comfortably, and focus on this breathing going in and out as a relaxing thought. With every exhale, repeat the word "relax."

As common as test anxiety is, it is very possible to overcome it. Make yourself one of the test-takers who overcome this frustrating hindrance.

Special Report: Additional Bonus Material

Due to our efforts to try to keep this book to a manageable length, we've created a link that will give you access to all of your additional bonus material.

Please visit http://www.mometrix.com/bonus948/gacebused to access the information.